In dedication to the new and emerging, the launching and relaunching entrepreneur with unrealized dreams. Here's to the inevitable evolution of you and your mission and your success and the impact you will make on this world.

CONTENTS

CHAPTER 1

Net Happiness, The True Bottom Line

If you are considering real estate as a career, are about to get your real estate license, or are currently a practicing REALTOR® but are not insanely happy with where you are at with your business, read this book.

I want you to read this book because I believe it can change your perception of really what it takes to succeed in this amazing business. For the experienced agent, it may be a simple course correction or a slight shift in priority. For the new agent, it can be a seriously valuable roadmap.

In business, we talk about net income as the top line and net profit as the bottom line.

I believe the true bottom line is net happiness.
Are you truly happy with your business and your life?

The thing with real estate career net happiness is that for many, it's an elusive, slippery slope. Success and momentum and client leads and cash flow here this month, missing in action the next. Happy then frustrated, confident then not, cash flow then cash tight. I have some theories around this.

One of my main theories is that an increase in sales tends to fix everything. I know, not an advanced business concept, but I've seen it in action for years. A frustrated agent, and all of a sudden they have three new clients, and now they're happy. That cycle of frustration, from skip-in-your-step back to unsure, is exhausting and all too common. For newly licensed agents, doing whatever you can to quickly gain three or ten clients and then the next three or ten makes all the difference in the world. Garnering an increase in sales *quickly* may be the secret sauce. Clients now, build later. Hence the title, *Success Faster.* I have other theories around this success formula, too, and we will work through them throughout this book.

Improve the trajectory, and overall enjoyment, of your business and your life, and you will change your world. Period. Change your world and you will set things in motion that inevitably will change another life. Divine. I believe we are all on this planet to participate in this process. My sacred mission is to help you do that.

There is an underlying premise here in *Success Faster*, and I'm pretty sure no one taught you this in real estate school. The premise is that the industry so heavily promotes the top 1% superstars that the bulk of agents in the middle end up tuning out the majority of industry advice and guidance. If you are a top 1% mega-mega-superstar agent, this is not your book (unless you mentor someone and need a tool or unless your little sister or neighbor or favorite client is about to get her real estate license, then you may want to engage her in this conversation).

Here is what you will get with *Success Faster*: authentic, relatable, practical, and actionable real advice and guidance for the launching or relaunching of a traditional real estate professional. You will get less of how to make the cover of *Realtor Magazine*, and more of how to have a solid business and life.

This book is for everyone who wants to succeed in the world of real estate. That especially includes those considering real estate as a career, newly licensed Realtors, Realtors who have yet to reach their goals, and Realtors in need of a reset or a simple calibration or course-correction. We will call these categories prelaunch, launch, and relaunch. Prelaunch is the maybe or soon-to-be Realtor, the launch is the newly minted Realtor, and the relaunch is the agent, however seasoned, who needs to (or is choosing to) hit the reset button in his or her business. Reset can be a beautiful thing, and *Success Faster* will act as the reset tour guide.

Some brokers have robust training and coaching programs to help the launching and relaunching agent. Other brokers, not so much. There are programs online and in person, programs that are free and those that are costly, programs that have been around for years and new options surfacing all the time. You could spend 24 straight hours on YouTube alone on the topic. You could spend thousands of hard-earned dollars on some of these programs. The body of real estate knowledge, advice, and direction is not one size fits all, and it certainly is not one budget fits all. Find the tools, programs, resources, and brokerage that work best for you, your life, your budget, and your business. *Success Faster* will help guide you in this process.

Success Faster will provide newcomers with a leg up on getting started faster, with insight into the mindset, skills, and panache it takes to get into a groove (and stay there) in this fast-paced, high-attrition business.

Success Faster will provide relaunchers with a fresh platform to reset and move forward, to recommit to the joy you experience when things are working nicely in your favor. You know that little skip in your step? We're going to tap into that. We will cover success stories, challenges, what to do, setting up your success plan, the habits that matter the most, what to say, how to garner clients quickly.

Success Faster can help. Let's take a closer look.

PRELAUNCH

You are considering real estate as a career, or are in the midst of moving in that direction. The fact that you have this book in your hands during your prelaunch phase is an indication of great things to come. You are a planner, you are forward thinking, you are starting a new chapter in your life.

A new chapter in your life...take that in for a minute. Whether in your twenties, your forties, or your sixties, a new license, a new direction, a new career, it's a new chapter...and that, in and of itself, is profound. Congratulations. Your new chapter (and your psyche and your family and your bank account) deserves a solid foundation, a solid launching pad. *Success Faster* will provide a framework for a successful start.

Start telling your story now, sharing your vision, passion, and motivation for why you are taking your life in this direction. Tell your story now so by the time you have your license and are ready to go, your world will already support you and align itself with your new path. Start your momentum now.

LAUNCH

You are a freshly minted Realtor in your first year or two. Congratulations, you have started a new chapter in your life. You may be the young kid starting out in the business, the retiree starting a new career, or the "employee" finally making the leap into self-employment. (You do know most Realtors are self-employed, right?) New life chapters, they're a big deal, and you owe yourself a pat on the back for having the wherewithal to get here.

The learning curve is steep; cash flow and your lead pipeline are everything. The first one to three months are the honeymoon phase of starting something new. The reality—that your real estate license school did not teach you how to thrive in this business—settles in relatively quickly. Mentors are critical. In most cases, you are now your own boss. Where do you capture your next client, your next ten clients? How do you ramp up? This book will serve as a launching pad to help you succeed and thrive in this amazing business.

RELAUNCH

The book is ideal for the relaunchers, Realtors who for some reason are starting over. It could be the maternity-leave parent re-entering the business, the agent who diverted onto a leadership path and is now back in production, or the agent who tasted momentum only to lose it or fail to recognize its elusive nature. Perhaps your financial trajectory has plateaued, or you are simply lacking the necessary cash flow to make your life work. Perhaps you simply need guidance getting to the next level, or desire a nudge or two in the right direction to regain your real estate swagger. Perhaps you're considering quitting, going back to being an employee, because your cash flow sucks. Please forgive the real estate analogy, but does your business simply need cosmetic work, fresh paint, or maybe new flooring and windows? Is it a fixer-upper or a complete tear-down? *Success Faster* can help.

I personally know relaunch well. I remember times in my business where the client leads just seemed to flow. I had a consistent supply of opportunity, and my phone was ringing. The pipeline was healthy, or so I thought. And then it would stop. And start again. And stop. The start was always energizing, pumped me up, good for my ego. The stop was defeating, frustrating, hard on cash flow, messed with my ego, messed with my head. Awesome shifted to not awesome. Flow shifted to lack. Swagger to doubt. I knew I had to level it out. I knew I had to run my business with more sophistication in order to achieve the stability, success, and peace of mind I so desired.

Success Faster will help if you are launching or relaunching your businesses, starting or restarting, or simply pushing through to the next level. There is no shame in restarting your business. I would never judge a restart, but I would seriously question staying with the status quo when it is not working. I have restarted many times. Restart is a beautiful thing, an intelligent move. If your business (or anything) is not working at a high level, start over. If you're not happy, start over. Burned out, start over. If cash flow is elusive, start over.

SHORT GAME VS LONG GAME

A truly successful launch or relaunch will be sustainable. One of the reasons many agents find themselves starting over is that they never built a reliable or sustainable client lead pipeline in the first place. They put so much attention on the short game of simply more sales and the next paycheck that they skipped the long game, the class on world-class service, exceptional market knowledge, superior contract prowess, and win-win negotiations. You have to do both short game and long game, quantity and quality, sales and value, all at the same time.

I recently attended a real estate conference, Inman Connect in San Francisco, where one of the speakers went off on this topic. James Becker, Fusion Growth Partners, said "Be the agent you would actually hire. Focus on real value, not sales techniques. If you do this, your next decade in business will be beyond your wildest dreams." He had observed that so many of the agents who achieved six-figure status in real estate often lost traction and their seat on the six-figure bus the longer they were in the business. He thinks they were spending too much time on short game (more leads, always more leads) versus long game (more value, more service, more impressive value-laden market knowledge).

In the short game, you are always chasing your next sale; in the long game, consumers will seek you out, friends will send their friends. Every seasoned Realtor knows that the repeat client and the referral lead are the best opportunity, the most cost effective, and a sign of a value-driven business.

A successful agent focuses on true value and delivery, and thus builds a sustainable pipeline of clients, repeat clients, raving fans, and referrals. Think of the large corporation who has both a large and competent sales force (the short game, the pipeline builders) and amazing product development, engineering, service, and delivery teams (the long game). If that corporate sales team cranks out the sales, but the product or delivery teams fail to deliver, then it's broken. You get the picture.

In *Success Faster*, we are going to walk the fine line between short game and long game, between gaining your next lead and client and sale quickly (this is important) and building competency and quality (this is critical and ethical). These two concepts are not oppositional. Rather, they must work in tandem. The short game, in any sales profession, is foundational. There is an old business adage: "sales fixes everything." But never at the expense of quality and sustainability. Short game success without long game quality and foundation is simply lousy business.

Success Faster is designed for any agent who is working to create (or recreate) a solid real estate business with a healthy client pipeline, predictable cash flow, and a life.

You've already started…you're reading this book. You're ready to take action. You're ready to make money. You're ready to build your life through the success of your real estate business. The book is practical, actionable, and may be just the thing you need to make this career choice work for you, to gain or regain your seat on the bus.

Success Faster will hit you with business insights, tips and action plans, what to say, how to build, and it includes a dose or two of tough love. There is a NOTES section in the back of the book intended as a place keeper for your aha's and your insights.

WORKING IT OUT IN THE MIDDLE

You may be wondering how this book is different from the hundreds of books, blogs, videos, and other online resources on the topic. You may be wondering how this book differs from what your brokerage delivers in the training, coaching, and mentoring arena. You may be wondering how this book varies from some of the world-class programs available in this great big real estate world. First, let me tell you what the book is not.

This is not a book of superstar centerfolds, what they did to get started, how big their marketing budgets are, what their plan is to expand into other cities, and how awesome they are today. With all due respect, those superstars are some amazing businesspeople who have worked their tails off to get where they are today, and many of them had humble beginnings. Some of them almost failed out of the business before they succeeded. While I will sprinkle in some impressive success factoids, the read will not be dominated by the top 1% super producers. Here's the deal; the top 1% has changed considerably over the years. The top 1% ten years ago is almost chump change today. Today's top 1%, they are running empires. Empire building, that's another book written by somebody else.

I have found there to be a tremendous need in the industry for advice and guidance for the agents who are working it out in the middle. If this speaks to you, you are in the right place.

Depending on your market, middle could be $3 million in sales, or middle could be $30 million in sales. Middle is simply the group of agents who are not beginners and are not the top rated in their market. The middle of the real estate pro rankings has some serious way-above-average talent.

I have read so many articles where the author bio says "I was top 1% in the country." Seriously, how many top 1% agents are out there, and is that the model and motivation and right approach for the 80% of the agents in the middle? My professional story is a story of a solid, competitive agent in the middle, working her way to success and sustainability, knowing I could do more and knowing I could have better bank, better balance, and a better life. I knew I was a good agent and I wanted more; not all, just more. I did not desire to be top 1%; I just wanted to achieve, and push my financial and life balance goals. I found myself constantly in search of the message and the messenger that spoke to my place in the world.

What the real estate industry needs more of is a voice that speaks to the bulk of agents fighting for stability and awesomeness in the middle. In 2016, Brad Inman of *Inman News* acknowledged the Everyday Realtor as the Person of the Year:

> *... shout-out to the entrepreneur, the young kid starting in the business, the individual who doesn't have a paycheck every two weeks, no benefits, 100% commission, the true entrepreneur. These extraordinary people earn a living without receiving a salary or even minimum wage. They are entirely commission-based—they wake up every morning without a paid job. They must dig deep and reach high to find the fortitude to keep it going. Theirs is not easy work. No one is paying for their health insurance, sick days, paid time off or maternity leave. No one buys them a computer, a cell phone or a company car.*

I ran a top 10% real estate practice in Austin, Texas. Besides an occasional dreamy thought, being in the top 1% club was never really my aspiration. I wanted a healthy bank account, a decent vacation fund, I wanted to make a difference in people's lives, and I wanted a life with some breathing room. Does this speak to you? From personal observation, I believe there are a lot of agents out there in this pack.

As my career progressed into leadership, coaching, and training, I became more and more enamored with the new and middle agents.

I found significant meaning and tremendous reward working with the new, emerging, launching, relaunching, pivoting agents in the middle of the pack.

Whether new and emerging, beginning or middle, getting the right things done is critical to moving forward. To support your forward progress, one of the key things you will find in *Success Faster* is action. Most chapters give you tasks, ACTION ITEMS designed to help you move toward client leads now, and tasks designed to build or improve your foundation. The key here is that as soon as you have more leads and a more consistent pipeline, most of your other problems will solve themselves. Life lesson, right? Fix the foundation and everything else seems to fix itself.

The other key that the book addresses is the reality of how you are showing up in the world. I have seen well-meaning, hard-working entrepreneurs completely sabotage their business because their energy is low, or they are trying to be someone they are not. The book spends some time on authenticity, and a tool I call your power score.

BORDERLINE OBSESSED

I am borderline obsessed with this topic, this real estate success and sustainability thing. I have spent hours and hours on the topic of new and emerging agent success, researching every possible resource and angle and best practice out there. I have trained and coached hundreds of new agents in the largest real estate office in the world. I have delivered and sat through training after training on the topic. I have spent countless hours consulting with agents who have traction, as well as agents who have little to no traction. I have found there to be a few critical differences among both agents who succeed and those who do not. We will explore these differences throughout the book.

My ultimate mission is to help you succeed. With the exception of real estate hobbyists, tinkerers, individual investors, and the clueless, everyone who chose to get a real estate license was making a conscious decision to change their life. In writing and delivering this book, I get to help you change yours. When this book is the difference maker for one agent, one family, one future, then I have succeeded.

Your success, my obsession.

FAST BEATS SMART

So let me explain the title, *Success Faster*, in a bit more detail. The theory behind this book (and my experience) is that acquiring clients *faster* may be THE biggest success differentiator.

Faster trumps smart.

Faster trumps talent.

Smart and talent will catch up, but the agents who gain clients and momentum faster will have all sorts of things working in their favor, and this will frustrate the heck out of the smarty-pants and the chronically organized. Let me paraphrase, hustle wins. Clients faster.

WARNING LABEL!

Real estate involves people's lives, money, and legal contracts. While fast and hustle are part of the business success formula, broker and mentor support go hand-in-hand until you have a dozen transactions under your belt. Be smart!

So what does that hustle look like? How do you gain clients quickly? *Success Faster* provides actionable steps you can take today to gain clients faster. Clients faster leads to gaining traction faster, which leads to all sorts of sexy things in your business ecosystem, which leads to more clients, which leads to you taking a decent vacation, and so on. It is a beautiful cycle of making things happen in your business and your world.

Success Faster is less of a pep talk and more of a roadmap, a to-do guide for gaining momentum. If you engage in the action, really, truly do the work outlined throughout the book, I would bank on your success.

First, let me tell you more of my story, and the various pivots—some more poetic than others—that got me to where I am today.

CHAPTER 2

The Art (And The Mess) Of The Pivot

My imaginary career-start headline: "Seduced by success, REALTOR® breaks records, achieves top honors, sets new standards, funds nonprofit animal rescue in two years, runs a marathon, takes long vacations, makes it look easy, writes a book."

My truth-o-meter career-start headline: "Seduced by success, perfectionist extrovert-leaning rosy glasses Realtor had no idea what she was getting herself into, restarts business multiple times, funds chicken farm in 15 years, stops running, makes it look easy, writes a book." More on the chicken farm later.

I have been in real estate since 1999. Based on industry standards, I had a good first year. Seduced by success, I had $3,798,315 in sales volume my first full year in the business. I have trained Rookies of the Year who did three or four times more volume than that, but at the time, in 2000, it was a solid, respectable first year. It was more money than I had been making in my previous career, I was having a blast, and this working from home on my own schedule thing was the greatest invention ever. I was professionally grinning from ear to ear.

And then I sold $3.3 million in real estate my second year, and $3 million my third year. I was sliding backwards. I realized I had no plan, was lacking focus, was being a lousy boss to myself, and that my business was running me. Honeymoon over. I had no control over my pipeline, had zero training on the concept of pipeline, my cash flow was completely unpredictable, I had little control over my *flexible* (air quotes) schedule, and my business was running me and my life. I was a stress bucket and needed solutions.

So I started over. Some sort of business intuition or personal fortitude kicked in, and I started over. That was my first significant pivot in my real estate career.

I can track seven significant pivots in my real estate career, and have absolutely lost count of all the minor pivots. Some of these were fluid, a bit of an art; some were more on the messy side. In looking back, I believe I pivoted a lot. As it turns out, business pivoting is a bit of a skill, a survival technique of sort. Two steps forward, one step back. Not always linear, sometimes sideways, sometimes messy. It's a bit of a business cha-cha-cha.

My story is not one of uber top 1% production. It is not one of mega team superstardom. Top 10% always felt like a good number. Top 20% is respectable in the business. My story is one of pushing through to make more money than I had ever made before, of pushing through to secure my future. I wanted security, I wanted cash flow, I wanted meaning in my professional endeavors. My story is one of being bound and determined to get balanced, get into the top 10%, and stay there. And then falling off, and then getting back, each time a bit smarter. It is a story that cycles from balance to out of balance, back to balance, and so forth.

The number of times I pivoted, reset, and a few times completely re-launched my business is a significant part of this story. Sometimes the best thing to do is simply start over. Or pivot.

Diet not working? Start over. Working out not working? Try something different. Relationship not working? Tweak. Or start over. Sales under target? Pivot. Sales way under target? Start over. Not happy? Evaluate and start over.

I find that most successful business owners, most successful real estate professionals, pivoted a lot or wish they had pivoted sooner. This is common. Some of the top agents in the country, the superstars, the megateams, I've seen hundreds of them onstage all telling similar stories of quite messy early years. I have heard the best of the best say they almost left the business, they almost left before they pivoted, they failed before they succeeded.

The business pivot topic is not new. There is a Forbes article from July 2015 on the business pivot that says: "According to one estimate, as many as 15-20% of startups pivot from their initial business plan. In some ways, pivoting a company can be like pressing the restart button on your laptop, and it can breathe new life into a failing venture." That 2015 Forbes article references a 2012 New York Times article on the topic of how startups often fail their way forward. It's the fail-forward concept of "...sometimes the first try doesn't go as planned."

I am a big fan of the restart button, and a big fan of the hit-the-reset-button approach to getting what you want. Not happy? Change something.

Let's take a closer look at my pivot record.

PIVOT 1: YEAR 3, VISION

I loved my first brokerage. It was a small boutique run by two dear friends, and they were generous in mentoring my start in the business. Former educators, the mentor thing came naturally to them. And I was a good student, a talented junior agent. With $3.8 million in sales volume in my first full year (all personally generated), I awarded myself the Rookie of the Year award. The problem with that self-assigned award is that, besides being self-assigned, I was the only rookie. No competition. So a bit of a fake award...but what I needed at the time.

As with many agents, it took me a year or two to begin to form the vision of what I really wanted with this new career. Did I want my own brokerage? Who did I want to be as a Realtor? How could I make the biggest impact? What sort of specializations interested me? What was I good at? What sort of customer experience did I want to provide for my clients? How could I bring more value? How would I attract the ideal client? How in the heck do you take time off in this business? Realistically, how much money could I make? What was I building, and how was I going to get there?

I came to the realization that I wanted a bigger platform to build on my vision. I was with a small brokerage, and they were, and still are, successful, professional, trustworthy, generous, good people. But I was itchy and my business was flat. I did not know how to get to the next level, and I'm not sure I asked. I felt the need to be exposed to different ways to do this thing called real estate. I felt insulated, and wanted to know how the rest of the world did real estate. I was curious about other successful Realtors. I wanted a bigger platform to create the customer experience I was starting to piece together. Because of how I learn, I came to the realization that I needed to be around as many top producers as possible. So in the sophomore year of my real estate career, I moved my business to the biggest game in town.

This was not an easy decision for me. I hate disappointing anyone. I am a nice, youngest child, Midwest girl, and I lost sleep over disappointing my business partners—my friends who believed in me, who had mentored me for two years. But I made the business decision. I pivoted.

PIVOT 2: YEAR 8, TEAM

With a new focus and a huge training push, I pulled my business out of the slide, hitting $5 million, then $7 million, then $9 million over the next three to four years. And I was killing myself. I was working all the time. I needed help, I needed leverage. So the second major pivot in my real estate career was building a team. It started with an assistant (always start with an assistant), and then a buyer's agent. I was learning how to leverage, and how to incorporate that into my business.

PIVOT 3: YEAR 10, ACQUISITION

In 2009, I had the opportunity to acquire another agent's business. She was a top agent in my office, and she had a unique opportunity to move her family back to California. To make that happen, she needed an Austin business partner to adopt her client relationships, and I was the right match. A bit like a second marriage and growing your family. I gained a seriously talented buyers agent in the acquisition. I started my team over.

The team lineup changed four or five times over the years. To be brutally honest, I was really good at real estate and sort of okay running a team. I see this a lot in the general Realtor population… good at real estate, not great running a business. Being a good boss, running the team, was not my strongest suit. But the team members were good, smart, hardworking people, and we all liked each other, so it worked. In hindsight, the models that exist today for building and running a team, for being a good real estate boss, are amazing compared to what I was working with at the time. But again, a pattern re-emerged, and I was working all the time. (Hint: look for your patterns.) I was out of balance and seeking direction for my team. So I hired a coach, an interim CEO of sorts.

PIVOT 4: YEAR 12, BE CAREFUL WHAT YOU ASK FOR

I believe there are magical times in life when the stars align and opportunities and blessings show up in your path. Without fail, these blessings only show up when you are ready, and in my experience, when you finally have the clarity and wherewithal to ask.

In October of 2010, I was seriously restless and had a meaningful conversation with my business coach. Typically, my conversations with my coach were specifically business-related: accountability, goal progress, obstacle maneuvering, mindset tweaks. Occasionally the coaching conversation was deeply personal. As it turns out, this particular conversation was personal and pivotal, and I tell this story all the time.

I told her I had two very distinct goals for the next year. Goal one, get my life back in balance. I felt like I was in the midst of, or at risk of, a self-imposed implosion. I seemed to have misplaced my happiness, and stress was kicking my butt. And goal two, increase my business. In that order. Happiness, health, and balance first, business second. I had profound clarity on these goals and I put them out there.

And a profound thing happened.

Seriously, the very next day, within twenty-four hours of this deeply personal and pivotal coaching conversation, I get a call from my Team Leader (similar to a managing broker). A leadership position had opened up and I was a possible candidate. I had the opportunity to take on the Director of Career Development position in the largest real estate office in the world—at the time, the largest by agent count and volume of real estate sales. (A little precursor here, I had been voluntarily running the Education Committee in this office for years, working closely with the Director to drive that program.) I asked the universe for balance, and this was the very loud answer, the show-up-in-my-voicemail-within-24-hours answer.

All the lights went on. Super big pivot.

This was a coveted coaching position within the Keller Williams Realty franchise system. This type of opportunity rarely surfaces, and I ran with it. I quickly partnered my business with another top agent in the office and started working on that transition.

PIVOT 5: YEAR 17, CRASH

My go-to analogy for stress repetitively showing up in my world is that I am a sprinter, not a marathoner. Literally and figuratively. I prefer the short distance to the long. When I take on something, I go full-on, pedal to the metal, and I keep going. And I have a tendency to say "yes" a lot, I take things on. This bodes well for the quarter mile, and is a failure ticket for the marathon.

I was running the largest new agent training program in the country. For five years, I helped nearly 150 brand-new agents each year get their start in real estate. This was super meaningful work; I helped agents change their lives. And I oversaw the overall training effort in this big office. I was sprinting. And saying yes a lot. Sprint, yes, sprint, yes. And I hit a wall.

I landed at the cardiologist. I am a healthy, sporty, trim, 50-something and my heart was racing, my chest was tight.

I remember specifically how it happened. I was at a coaching workshop just outside Austin with about 300 coaches, trainers, and industry leaders from around the country. I remember the exact seat I was sitting in—middle left aisle about ten rows back, blue backpack, black suit jacket, shiny silver shoes (I have a shoe thing). And something was off. I was pretty sure it was not right for a healthy, sporty, well-hydrated gal to have a racing heart and tightness in her chest. I tried meditating in my seat. I tried breathing exercises. I ate a healthy snack, drank some water. And it persisted.

So I walked out shaking. I was practically in tears. I knew a lot of the folks running the conference, so I asked for help. In the back hallway, I told someone that I was having trouble breathing. They immediately summoned one of the top coaches at the conference, my former health coach. When she set eyes on me, she literally had to look twice, because when she got the message that someone at the conference was having chest tightness and breathing issues, frankly I think she expected to encounter an older, heavier, or unhealthy conference attendee and I didn't fit the profile. I remember the questioning look on her face. I think the first word out of her mouth was simply, "Julie?" as she looked quizzically around, to see if there was someone else standing nearby having breathing issues.

Fast forward, it was not a heart attack. I get to the hospital, pass all the tests with flying colors, get assigned to a cardiologist for more tests. Everything checks out fine. Turns out that sprinting and sprinting and sprinting is not sustainable. Go figure. I was exhausted and stress was showing up in my body. I landed at the cardiologist again five months later, same thing. Same symptoms, same test results, same diagnosis. It was a wakeup call. Something had to shift. Time to pivot.

So the next big pivot in this story is how I decided to go back to being a solo entrepreneur, formalize the Nelson Project training and coaching company, and finish writing this book.

PIVOT 6: YEAR 18, RELAUNCH

My training and coaching company had been part of my work for years. Helping real estate businesspeople grow their successful careers has been a longtime passion that fuels my inner fire. Now was the time to pull it all together and relaunch. In 2016, I generated the first published version of this very book, designed a couple online courses, became a contributing writer for Inman News, blogged, podcasted, spoke nationally, got my life and health back. And made very little money in the process. It was a bit of a sabbatical year. And I loved it.

As a bit of a side note, I want to make a comment on the sabbatical concept. I think we need more of this in our culture. I've done it twice. Academia prescribes it. Australia calls it a gap year. Europe practically shuts down in August. We are such a hardworking, driven society, and I have seen so many people whose work/life balance thing is not balanced at all. It's a challenge in real estate. Work, work, work. Disrespect the family, the kids, your health. Sprint, sprint, sprint. Skip meals. Sprint. And life flies by. And then you land at the cardiologist. If you can afford it, consider a sabbatical. It doesn't have to be a year—perhaps it's a month in Europe or a long RV trip with the kids. When you are about to relaunch, it is super valuable, if not critical, to get your head right, your health right, your priorities straight, catch your breath, reclaim your life. Relaunch with a solid foundation.

Back to my story.

I realized that I needed to redesign and boost my financial path. My spouse had recently retired at 53 from a 29-year teaching career, and we were taking a close look at our 10-year plan. It was very clear to me what I needed to do. I would continue some training, writing, and speaking, but what is it that I know how to do best? Real estate. With renewed vigor, health, and clarity, I relaunched my *real* real estate business in 2017.

As I write this book, I am relaunching my business, my real estate practice. If anyone can do it, the director from the one of the largest agent training programs in the country can.

True to form, I gave this relaunch a theme. Zero to ten in ten months (from $0 to $10M in sales). An aggressive goal, but doable for an experienced agent fresh off sabbatical with a vision, the right leverage, and best practices. Why 10? I was sure I could do $6M, could most likely do $8M, and $10M sounded like a nice stretch goal...and was catchy with the 10 months left in the year.

PIVOT 7: YEAR 18, CHANGING BROKERAGES

I did not see this coming. In the midst of my 2017 relaunch (pivot 6), I hired a coach. I had the 0-to-10-in-10 plan in place and moving along. I wanted (needed) some accountability to stay on pace, and help formulating my 5-year plan. The relaunch was working, but I was still trying to figure out the other pieces...my coaching practice, teaching opportunities, this book, creating a retirement plan, continuing to make a difference in the real estate world. I wanted help pulling all that together, and occasional conversations with my personal and professional besties—while valuable, insightful, and sometimes involving happy hour—were not resulting in the formulation of a clear plan. I laid out all of the pieces I was attempting to weave together, some more successfully than others, and we jumped in as a team to dissect and reassemble the tapestry into something I could wrap my arms and heart around. And an interesting thing happened.

I came to the realization that I was bumping into walls and ceilings at my current brokerage. Some self-imposed (my choices), some organizational evolution. I was either going to need to adapt or create a new solution. I had been adapting and then adapting some more, and realized I was morphing away from myself and playing small. Anyone who knows me knows I am not hard-wired to play small.

As I moved through this soul-searching business and personal re-evaluation exercise, I realized that the process was a tremendous amount of work. The work-through-your-stuff is heavy lifting for introspective-leaning, fiercely loyal types like me. For other folks who are all business, perhaps this type of exercise is natural, and you easily move onto another opportunity. For me, it took some time. I had an amazing 16-year run with Keller Williams Realty full of opportunity, a values-driven culture, and amazing people. But it was looking and feeling like the box maybe didn't fit anymore. Methodically, my coach helped me work through my noise and vision. One of the main benefits of doing that hard introspective work is that I fully vetted my needs, my thoughts, my 5-year plan... my resolve was rock solid, and I moved my 18-year license to a newer emerging technology-based brokerage, eXp Realty. New chapter!

In the How to Choose a Broker section of this book (Chapter 16), we will dissect different options and how to approach that professional choice: starting your career or moving your license mid-career.

PIVOT 8: TBD, MY TRUTH-O-METER

My truth-o-meter is that my Pivot #8 is TBD: To Be Determined. Late in the process of writing *Success Faster*, and after much introspection (believe me, write a book and you'll be in introspection overload, years' worth of introspection wrapped into hundreds of hours and months and months of brain space!), it had me wondering what my next pivot might be. Why wouldn't there be another pivot out there? What other opportunities will surface? My mindset could shift. What lovely sabbatical may present itself? I could win the lottery. (I could!) I dream of an RV trip. (Often.) A month of skiing has been on the bucket list for some time. (It will happen.) So I add Pivot #8 as a place keeper for my next move or opportunity. And how lovely to know that it is there, that place keeper for something awesome, something new, something unknown.

So back to the truth-o-meter career start headline, I am writing this book for you. I am writing this book for the beginning and middle Realtor who has a dream. I am writing this book for the relaunching Realtor who has a vision. I am writing this book for the pivoting professional. I am writing this book for the real estate pro who has not yet found her groove. I am writing this for the agent who is a bit over the overabundance of mega-mega-mega superstar agent advice out there that applies to almost no one. (Really, if you have a $30k per month budget for marketing, mailing, and lead generation, this is not your book.) If you are that Realtor (or Realtor-to-be) who has the vision of creating some amazingness in your life through real estate career success, then this book is for you. Regardless of the size, shape, or color of your sales goals (3, 5, 10, 20 million…it's your goal, own it, and don't let anyone tell you you are not thinking big enough!), I write this book for anyone who has pivoted and judged themselves for it, or anyone who thinks they may need to pivot and is judging that as some sort of failure, setback, or falling short. Pivot is brilliance in action.

Let's take a closer look at how *Success Faster* will help you get on track to building something amazing in your life.

CHAPTER 3

INTRODUCTION, SOME THINGS THEY NEVER
TOLD YOU

CREATE SOMETHING AMAZING IN YOUR LIFE

When you made the decision to start in real estate, whether part-time or full-time (more on that later), you were making the decision to change your life. You realize that, right? Any new career choice is a choice for your future. Any new career choice, new career beginning, is you making a huge move toward your future. When you started in real estate, the day you decided to get your license, the day you actually got your license, the day you walked in your broker's door, the day you told your best friend what you wanted to do, you were making the decision to create some awesomeness in your world.

You made the decision to leave the safety, the financial safety and ceiling of the traditional workforce, and enter this amazing business. You made the decision to enter this business that, frankly, is a bit easy to get into, and much harder to stay.

In this book, we will plow into techniques and best practices that are designed to help you succeed in real estate, designed to help you gain clients and momentum quickly, designed to help you stay and thrive, designed to help you create something amazing in your life, designed to help you have the courage to pivot. *Success Faster* is practical and actionable, and is designed to help you get a leg up in an amazing business that, frankly, has a high fallout rate.

But there are some things they never told you in real estate school. Let's take a look.

CHALLENGES TO GETTING STARTED (OR RESTARTED)

Let's get the bad news out of the way fast. Statistics for first-year REALTOR® success are abysmal.

It is a common industry belief that the likelihood of a newly licensed Realtor still being in the business one or two years later is around ten percent. Simple math tells us that one out of every ten newly licensed agents will actually remain in the business.

I am not sure I fully buy into that statistic. I have spent hours trying to find the source of that widely-held number, the one out of ten success thing. I even e-mailed back and forth with NAR (the National Association of Realtors) researchers. NAR knows that the industry throws around this statistic like popcorn at a baseball game, but they said it did not come from them. I am a bit skeptical of the 90% attrition position. I am skeptical because there are so many licensees around the country that do other things besides full-on traditional real estate sales. There are property managers, administrators, and part-timers. But even if that attrition number is closer to, let's say, an 80% dropout rate, it's a daunting number.

It is my personal mission to increase that retention percentage, to positively impact the professional landscape, to increase the odds of your success in this business. It is my mission for you to be part of the ten or twenty percent who make this into a viable, sustainable, and rewarding business. Ultimately, my mission— and the mission of most industry trainers and coaches around the world—is to move the needle on that success quotient. I feel an obligation to participate in that success effort.

What are some of the reasons for this sobering statistic? I personally think it comes down to these five things: ease of licensure, unrealistic expectations, cash flow, being a good boss, and energy. I'll expand here a bit, and throughout the book in significantly more detail, on how you can overcome these potential hurdles.

ONE: Ease of Licensure

In most states, it is very easy to get a real estate license. Almost too easy. Fill out an application, pay some money, take four or five or six classes online (none of which are called How to Succeed in Real Estate), pay a little more money, pass a state exam, a national exam, and a background check, maybe some fingerprints, pay a little more money to join a board and MLS, find a broker, and tada! You're in business! Now what?

This happens in many industries. I asked my favorite doctor, my go-to doc who runs her own small practice, did they teach you how to run a business in med school? No. I have asked my therapist friends the same question; did they teach you how to run a business in your masters or PhD program? No. I asked my massage therapist. No. I asked my nephew, Ian, who is a professional chef in Chicago. One class. You get the picture.

In your real estate classes, did they teach you how to run a real estate business? In real estate school, did they teach you how to generate leads and build a healthy pipeline? In real estate school, did they teach you what to say when someone says "Why should I hire you?" or "I am interviewing three agents," or "How's the market?" No, they did not. Or that class was optional. Your real estate school taught you contracts (although they missed nuance and negotiation), finance, legal, and ethics, and how to pass a state and national exam.

TWO: Unrealistic Expectations

Your real estate license classes taught you how to pass an exam. You learned real estate ethics, real estate law, real estate contracts, and real estate finance. You may have learned some marketing. All very important things. But your pre-license real estate school missed some very important and foundational things.

Your classes did not teach you how to attract and retain clients, how to build a pipeline of qualified clients, or how to run a business. Additionally, your pre-license classes most likely did not cover any sort of financial model instruction, including expense and profit targets. Arguably, I would like to see Business and Sales 101 added to the pre-license course requirements. Newly minted Realtors show up eager to jump into their new business and realize, very quickly, that it costs money to run a real estate business, and attracting clients is harder and slower than they thought.

And what about your broker? Does your broker teach you how to run a good business? The old real estate brokerage model, which still exists today, does not produce business owners; it simply produces salespeople who are dependent upon their broker. Know what you are getting from your broker and know that you need a lot more training in your first couple years.

Today's real estate model is different...you must learn to be a good businessperson. Did anyone tell you, before you got your license, that you were in a lead generation business first and a real estate business second? Did they teach you about CRMs and a pipeline and an efficient follow-up system? If so, you're one of the lucky ones. If not, you learned that super fast, right?

THREE: Cash Flow

These unrealistic expectations can lead to the third reason, cash flow. Everything in real estate, every payday, is sixty to ninety days out. That means that the work you are doing today will result in your paycheck in two to three months. Conversely, the work you do *not* do today will not result in a paycheck in two to three months. The work you do (or do not do) in the fourth quarter will show up (or not) in your bank account the first quarter, your first quarter work will show up in your bank account the second quarter, and so on. If it is new construction, that paycheck can be nine months out. If it is a commercial contract, six to twelve months is not uncommon. If a brand new agent starts on January 1, will she have a paycheck in March or April? It depends on what she is doing in January.

If an agent is slow to start, or is cautious or lacking confidence or is a bit of a perfectionist, that agent may not have a client lead in January. Or the agent may have two or three leads, but none of them convert yet to an active client. I just closed with a client that I have been communicating with, regarding her lease property, for eight years. You get the picture. Cash flow, or the lack thereof, is very real for most new agents. Agents who start in the business with very little cash reserves basically have a cash flow problem on day one. Cash is king and sales solve everything.

FOUR: Bossy

And the fourth reason, in my opinion, for the abysmal first-year success rate for Realtors is failure to be a good boss. This is a huge topic worthy of its own book. So many agents are not holding themselves accountable to a strict schedule and a reliable daily lead generation effort. I will dive deeper on this topic, but for now, let's agree on a couple of things. First, the good news about your new career choice is that you are your own boss. The bad news? You are your own boss.

FIVE: Power Score

The fifth challenge may be your energy, your confidence, how you are showing up in the world. I call this your power score, and we will dive deep into that later. Here is the basic premise...you are in the people business. You are in the business of having conversations with people about real estate. This takes a certain amount of energy, of people-attraction juju. Does being around and engaging with people bring you energy or completely zap you? How well do you adapt when someone's style is different than yours? Do you like to be in the mix or do you prefer solitude, quiet, and an impressive spreadsheet?

When I was in the training director seat, I had new agents in my office all the time. I could usually read someone's power score within minutes. The power score walked in the room before their seat hit the chair. How were they carrying themselves? What was their energy? How was their eye contact?

This is not an introvert-extrovert thing. I have trained introverts whose power score was high; I have trained extroverts who seemed to misplace their confidence in the newness of the situation. In early chapters, we will dive into taking inventory on how you're showing up in the world. As with any big task, goal, new chapter, starting a new business, training for a marathon, preparing for grad school, or planning a family, taking inventory on where you're at in comparison to probably where you need to be can make all the difference in the world. Do you need to change to accomplish that big task, to become who you want to be? Or is it an enhancement of who you already are?

The good news is that you can do this. You can do this, and it is a super cool business with limitless opportunity. The good news about your success? It's what it will do for your life, your family, your independence.

Your success in your real estate career? It will change the trajectory of your life.

Let's take a look at some changed lives, see if you relate to any of these stories.

REAL AGENT STORIES

JULIE: Thought About Real Estate For Years

Before I got into real estate, I had a career in high-tech. The high-tech thing, it chose me; I did not choose it. I was the liberal arts grad in a sea of engineers, and was lacking a vision of where I wanted to go, of how I wanted to live my life. It was a good company with good people. I was paid well (or so I thought), and had amazing travel opportunities. In a growing company where I was a bit of a utility player, I seemed to have a new title every six to twelve months. I was a leaf in the career stream, flowing downstream with few navigational tools, taking on whatever came my way with little vision of what was around the next bend or really what I wanted. I was lacking a steering device and a compass. I was beginning to think that my career path, my professional life, would never fill my soul, that professional bliss was not in my cards. I was starting to settle. And I was restless.

And then I got laid off. After eight years. The layoff day was a good day (I remember it well) because that is when I turned the corner toward real estate. I turned the corner to the rest of my life. I turned the corner toward doing something that I actually loved.

I had thought about real estate off and on for years, but had been talked out of it a couple times. And besides, I had a good job, so why replace good income, opportunity, and benefits with a 100% commission entrepreneurial endeavor that was harder than it looked? And get this—at age sixteen, I took a test that rated me low on entrepreneurial skills, and for crying out loud, that actually stuck with me. What age sixteen message do *you* need to dump? I have met a lot of people who relate to this story.

When I finally decided to get started, it was as if all the lights went on. Everything finally clicked, everything was in place to make this happen. I was about to have a career that spoke to me at a deep level, a career that made sense. I was no longer that leaf in the corporate stream. I was in charge of my professional life. I had never felt this way before. I never before had the courage to be self-employed (age sixteen baggage), and now here it was, right in front of me. It completely changed the trajectory of my life.

STEPHANIE: Newly Divorced Mama Bear

Newly divorced with two teenage daughters in a high-end neighborhood, Stephanie needed solutions fast. With a medical sales background, she knew how to talk to people. Stephanie needed a financial solution for her family, and she needed to show her daughters that women can be professionally successful. She intended to set a tone with her daughters that the divorce was not a setback, it was a launching pad. She needed to show her daughters what empowerment looked like, needed to show courage in the face of change, that starting over could be a very good thing.

Stephanie crushed it her first year. Stephanie was all mama bear, fierce and fearless and powerful and clear.

You see, Stephanie was not the top of her real estate class; she had to work harder to learn the business. She took most of my training classes twice. But she ran circles around some of the brainiacs because of her clarity and gumption. Angela Lee Duckworth calls this *grit* in her TED Talk: "Grit: the power of passion and perseverance." Stephanie had grit, and her real estate career changed her life and laid a new foundation for her daughters.

WILLIAM: Building A Life

Single father with two small boys. When William first walked into my office, our first coaching session, I had a hard time reading him. Either his energy was a bit low, or perhaps he was a quiet observer. He was pleasant, soft spoken, good eye contact, a bit unclear on his direction, a man of few words, a bit loose on his ability to name a goal. He wasn't sure where he wanted to take his real estate career or what it would take for him to go full-time.

There was something compelling about William, something that made me think his well ran deep. I soon learned that not only would William talk to anyone (he is currently working with someone he met at the gas station), his roots in east Austin, his family ties, were extensive. His parents, his brothers and sisters (eight kids!), knew everyone in the rapidly changing and gentrifying east Austin. William had connections that some agents only dream of. Every possible community leader, every auto shop, hair salon, restaurant, Little League coach—someone in William's family knew someone, and they all looked out for each other. They had learned, from poverty in the early years to family crisis later on, that they needed each other, and that family and community were everything.

Identify what you're good at, identify your assets, identify your wheelhouse, and double down. For William, his wheelhouse was his network in one specific geographic area. In his first year, William did $3 million in volume as a part-time agent. He is on track his second year, full time, to do $6.5 million and is working on his second flip. His goal for year three is $10 million, three flips, and getting those two young sons into the best schools possible.

MELANIE: VP Level Marketing Pro

Marketing pro and former VP of Marketing for national e-commerce leaders, Melanie had an impressive 25-year career in Dallas. But a couple things were happening in Melanie's world that were causing her to reassess. She was consistently working eighty hours a week, and her father was aging in Austin; he was declining.

For years, Melanie had thought about relocating back to Austin, but VP-level and director-level marketing positions were few in Austin and plentiful in DFW. When the personal pull finally outweighed her high-end resume, Melanie bit the bullet and moved back to Austin.

Melanie had been a real estate junkie for years. She studied homes and design and the market and pricing in her spare time. She knew as much as some experienced agents. I had been telling her, for years, that real estate may be the solution to her next professional chapter, that a real estate career could free her from the corporate marketing world and create her Austin solution.

Melanie's real estate decision was a gradual one. She kept having short-term, high-level marketing opportunities through her various professional connections. She would start moving toward real estate, then have an opportunity to do a six-month marketing gig for big bucks. Then move a little more toward real estate, and one more corporate project would show up in her inbox. Not a bad problem to have, right? But Melanie wanted something more and different, and eventually went full-on with real estate.

SAM: 60-something Non-profit Executive

Sam had a successful career as a non-profit executive. His LinkedIn profile reads like a laundry list of getting things done: business operations management, strategic leadership, market development, process enhancements, client relations. Married, two teenage sons, silver-haired, a bit nerdy, a serious punster… everyone likes Sam and you want him on your team. But Sam's non-profit career hit a bump in the road, a bump called funding, and Sam found himself needing solutions. At the time, the funding environment for big non-profits created an oversupply of qualified director-level candidates. The resume-to-opportunity ratio was seriously lopsided in favor of the non-profit, and lacking for the candidates. So Sam turned to real estate in Austin, one of the most robust economies in the country.

With Sam's confidence, fearlessness, and people skills, he gained traction in real estate pretty quick. Give him a task, he would do it. Show him the best practices, he would jump in. Put him in the toughest training program you offer (the one that is competitive to get into), and he excelled. He had enough of a training and HR background that he trusted the training programs and best practices recommendations. He assumed those programs had teeth and proven records, so he simply did everything that he was taught, without hesitation. He was the best student...no ego, ready to emulate the top agents, willing to run with the industry standards.

Right away when he started, he was exposed to some of the top agents in Austin, Texas, and saw that many of them and their teams were following the model of hitting the phones first thing every day. He embraced the foundational principle of more conversations equals more business. Sam quickly developed mad phone skills and was cranking out calls for two to three hours every day. Most importantly, he was authentic, not salesy.

These stories and your story...some are unique and some are common life changes and choices. Your story represents the foundation of your start, the lens on your vision, the beginning of your path. We will get back to these vignettes later in the book for an update on how these agents are doing a few years into their careers. For now, let's look at one of the basic premises of *Success Faster*.

QUICKLY

Grit is passion and perseverance for very long-term goals. Grit is having stamina. Grit is sticking with your future, day in, day out, not just for the week, not just for the month, but for years, and working really hard to make that future a reality. Grit is living life like it's a marathon, not a sprint. ... What I do know is that talent doesn't make you gritty. Our data show very clearly that there are many talented individuals who simply do not follow through on their commitments. In fact, in our data, grit is usually unrelated or even inversely related to measures of talent.

— Angela Lee Duckworth, Grit: the power of passion and perseverance, April 2013 TED Talks

So how do you succeed in this business? By following the models and getting into action quickly. The bigger picture includes client experience, service, relationships, systems, marketing, market knowledge, and how you are contributing to your community. These bigger picture items are key, and represent the long game of surviving and thriving in this business. In this book, we are working closely with the short game of gaining clients quickly. The faster you gain clients, your short game, the faster you will get on your feet (or back on your feet). Clients quickly.

Pause for just a moment and write this down in your notes, or highlight it…clients quickly. Heck, write it out one hundred times. Say it out loud. Put a sticky note on the bathroom mirror. This is a foundational principle of this book, a foundational principle of business success. It's all about building your client pipeline quickly. If you are in retail, it's about getting people through the door. If your business is online, it's about getting click-throughs. In your real estate career, it's building a pipeline of client leads. Quickly.

Let's use my 0-to-10-in-10-months relaunch as an example. I knew that to successfully relaunch—and having a lot of people observe that relaunch (the pressure was on to succeed)—I needed to feed my pipeline quickly. I could not waste time. I knew my systems and tools and software and marketing would all happen quicker with a client in hand; clients first, systems second. The systems-then-clients approach would be too slow.

If you have a big corporate background, a big marketing background, are super detail and systems oriented, are an engineer type or a spreadsheet junkie, or are double-dipped in the talent department… then beware. Your natural tendency (or one that was built into you in the corporate world) will be to organize the heck out of your new business. Remember the Stephanie story earlier in this chapter? You are smarter and more experienced than Stephanie, but she is going to run circles around you because she is gritty and is building her pipeline while you work on your marketing plan.

Clients first. In my relaunch, I needed to simply hustle and find my first ten leads and clients quickly. And then my next ten. This simply involved having meaningful conversations with the key people in my life, with my professional friends and clients, with my connected and influential friends, with my Realtor network around the country.

And not letting any of my spreadsheets get in the way. Quickly. Five months in, I have $6M in the pipeline. It's a solid start.

You can succeed in this high-attrition business by gaining clients quickly.

If you are just getting started in the business, then it's your first ten clients. Quickly. If you are year two, year three, year ten, re-starting, re-booting, relaunching, then it's your next ten. Quickly.

You are always working on your next ten clients.

More clients, quickly, will resolve most problems in your business. Half of the chapters in this book will tackle the specifics of clients quickly. Starting with the very next chapter, the book outlines specific actions you can take *now* to make this happen in a more expeditious manner than what you are currently experiencing.

I see quite a few agents not gain much traction in their first year, and then super take off in year two, sometimes year three. This delayed momentum, while common, has one significant caveat: cash flow. Some agents can afford a sluggish first year, others not at all.

Because of cash flow, and definitely because of mindset, you absolutely need to be in the momentum club. Get in that club and stay there. Let's take a look at some agents who joined that club very quickly at the start of their careers.

CHAPTER 4

Success Stories...How Did These Rookie Sensations Kill It In Year One?!

I attend a lot of real estate conferences, and my favorite sessions, the speakers and panels I seek out the most, are those that feature the rookies of the year, the amazing out-of-the-box successes, the momentum grabbers, the freshman freaks. Refreshingly, most of these freshmen MVPs are humble, not salesy. In most all cases, they're authentic, in that their success was derived primarily from something close to home, something very close to their true selves. Let's take a closer look at some of these success stories. A couple of these successful agents hit it way out of the park, while a couple simply owned a solid start worthy of attention. Most of the names escape me, but their stories remain embedded in my brain.

ROOKIE OF THE YEAR PROFILES

The Minister Guy In Mississippi: One Call Per Day

This 30-something's real passion, his mission, was coaching and training pastors. He helped ministers and churches bring more people in. He started in real estate because he needed a flexible financial solution that would fund his mission. Real estate was not the end, it was the means. And here was his key: he knew everyone.

Some REALTORS® are phone volume freaks; this guy, seriously, he made one real estate lead gen phone call per day. One. And each daily real estate lead gen phone call typically resulted in an appointment. His script was something like, "In order to continue making an impact on churches and ministers in our area, I have to have three real estate appointments every week with someone who may need my services. Who do you know who is thinking of buying or selling, and will you make the introduction, ask them to meet with me?" It worked. Rookie of the Year finalist.

The Door-Knocker in Canada: New Shoes Every Three Months

This 30-something guy used to sell air conditioners door-to-door in Toronto or Vancouver, somewhere cold. ACs in Canada. His previous sales career was solely door-knocking. He was used to going door-to-door for eight hours a day. He said he wore through a new pair of shoes every 90 days. He was the top AC sales guy in his company. Knocking on doors was all he knew how to do. When he realized how he could take his current activity and seriously increase his paycheck, seriously increase the ROI on a pair of shoes, he jumped. When he learned that the lead generation benchmark for a top producer in real estate was three to four hours per day—in other words, door knocking for half the time he was accustomed to, half the shoes, half the doors with a higher paycheck—he was all in. Mr. Canadian door-knocker was a National Rookie of the Year finalist.

The Investor in Vegas: Soft Spoken

This 50-something guy was mild and soft-spoken, and had been personally investing in real estate for years. On the side from his full-time casino job, he had rentals and flips, and his friends and colleagues regularly asked him for help, help to find the deals, partnering on flips, negotiating with a FSBO (since this is the first FSBO reference, I'll define for the new folks … for sale by owner). He was creating a healthy portfolio, and was beginning to help his family and friends do the same. The writing was on the wall. He had zero marketing budget, was low-tech, definitely not salesy. He was the smart, nice guy who people trusted. Rookie of the Year finalist.

The Teacher in South Dakota: Home Every Day at 3

This 40-year-old mother of three was tired of teaching and wanted to meet her kids at the bus. I've always said there is a teacher or two or three out there right now in every state who, five years from now, will be a top producing agent in their town.

Teachers make great Realtors. They're hard-working, know everyone, and negotiate their way through every day. Yes, the skills a teacher learns in managing twelve- year-olds, and parents, and administrators come in handy in real estate. Most teachers I know, and I'm married to one, have personal fortitude beyond their years.

So this gal in South Dakota, her price point, the average price of a home in her area, was much lower than Mr. Door-Knocker Canada and Mr. Investor Vegas. She sold twice as many homes as those guys. Her key was really two things: her hustle, and she knew everyone.

And she caught the veterans off guard. While the veteran Realtors in Sioux Falls or Rapids (or what is the capital of South Dakota? I forget what town she was in), were cruising on their reputations, she started running circles around them, and they were not even aware of that until her sign started showing up more than theirs. She hired an assistant early on because she was innately aware that she needed to spend most of her time face-to-face with buyers and sellers. And it was non-negotiable that she would be home with her kids at 3:00 PM...her clients understood this. She would not allow herself to get buried in the deets, and she was committed to having a schedule that kept her priority on her family. Rookie of the Year finalist.

The High-end in LA: Spending Money to Make Money

Every year, it seems there is a Rookie of the Year finalist who is super high-end. A talented rookie who goes after the multimillion-dollar market right out of the box. None of the "oh, I have to earn my stripes in the middle before I venture into luxury" mindset. Often, these luxury rookie superstars are already in that genre of wealth, a sort of real estate silver spoon.

I already know what you're thinking. You think these multimillion-dollar price point lucky dogs have it easy, that they only need a deal every other month to rank as a top producer, that there is more luck and family tree involved than talent and hard work. You think that by some unnatural chain of events, they got to list Oprah's estate, end of story. Not this 30-year-old's success story.

Mr. High-end in LA knew he wanted this market, and knew he had to have top-notch, high-end, expensive marketing and support to make it happen. Mr. High-end in LA spent a lot of money to make a lot of money. Rookie of the Year finalist.

The International In NYC: Power Package

This 40-something female phenomenon in Manhattan was European, drop-dead gorgeous, had some sort of advanced degree in international business. She dressed to kill. She was a power package in high heels and went after one very specific market, international buyers. She was multilingual (so American of me to point that out, like that is actually a resume highlight, when *most* Europeans are multilingual) and did 100% of her marketing attracting international buyers online. Yes, high price point and a very narrow focus. Rookie of the Year finalist.

The FSBO Guy: 21 in 3 Months

Had 21 for-sale-by-owner listings within three months of being licensed. FSBO, it's all he did. Narrow focus. I do not remember anything more about him. I simply remember that FSBO is all he did, and he had 21 of them signed up for his services within three months. Rookie of the Year finalist.

I have shelves full of notes from real estate conferences. Stacks of notebooks, blog articles, plus a 145-page running journal of notes and industry insights. In fact, that 145-page running journal was this book in its infancy. Think you have a book in you? Start journaling or blogging on the topic every day and see where you're at in six months. Fortunately, that journal is searchable, and I was able to resurrect the Rookie of the Year gems, advice, and words of note from some very successful first-year agents and insights from endless hours spent on blogs and webinars and observing agents get their start.

As you can see from the stories above, these success stories come from all walks of life, with varying journeys, specialties, and interests. The success stories represent all ages, from a few knock-your-socks-off millennials who killed it online, to the hustling 30-something Canadian door-knocker, to the humble soft-spoken 50-something investor in Vegas, to the international specialist in Manhattan, to the former teacher and the hometown preacher boy who knows everyone in his west Mississippi town. From these stories and my journals and notebooks, I selected a handful of rookie success gems. Here is a simple collection of difference-makers, course-correctors, and aha-injectors, direct from the rookie stars, that made a big difference for someone:

- It started with mindset.
- I ask this all the time: "Who have you talked to in the last 30 days that has mentioned real estate?"
- Expect more referrals from your top 25 people and treat them accordingly.
- My biggest mistakes: time management and fear of signing the buyer agreement.
- No one told me my first listing could not be a $2 million mansion.
- I knew that I was simply going to attempt to out-hustle everyone and I prepared my family for an intense year.
- My broker told me I had to sign a new client every week.

So that's what I did. For eight straight weeks I signed a client every week. And then on the ninth or tenth week I did not. So I sheepishly went to my broker to ask for help and he said that no one signs a new client every week...I just told you that to motivate you.

- I was home every day at 3 to meet my kids off the bus because that was my job too. This was non-negotiable with my clients and they understood.

Look for more rookie gems scattered throughout the book. When you find a gem that works specifically for you, a message that causes you to pause, advice that seriously captures your attention, a quote or comment that is simply custom-designed for where you are right now or tailor-made for where you are going, then pause for a minute. Write it down. That one message, that one idea, that moment of clarity could be the one thing that shifts your mindset and your business to the next level.

Throughout this book, keep a keen eye out for your aha's, your break-through gems. I recommend that you take notes, keep a log, a journal of sorts. Your journal will begin to serve as a roadmap, an easily referenced collection of business insights: *your* business insights. One of my goals is that your insights, your aha's and takeaways from the book, will be the catalyst for your next wave of momentum and, ultimately, a key tool for you creating awesomeness in your business and life.

CHAPTER 5

Get the RIGHT Mindset and Get Started

Your mindset will make or break you. Every day. Make sure your mindset points you, and keeps pointing you in the right direction every day. Get it now. Keep it up. Train your brain muscles to have THIS mindset: I came here to succeed. Period. I will do what it takes to create my success ON PURPOSE.

Your mindset is your foundation, and just like a building needs a solid foundation (yes, a construction analogy in a real estate book… seems appropriate), so does your career start or restart. Let's cover a few foundational concepts as we build your success plan.

SUCCESS MINDSET IS KEY

Someone told me this in my first year in the business…that 20% of the agents do 80% of the business and you need to be in that top 20%. So how do you do that? You work smarter and harder and faster than the crowd. More specifically, you must be very purposeful in creating a steady flow of client leads, and consistent with your attention to building a solid client pipeline, and persistent with the systems that make that happen. Leads, pipeline, systems. We will work with this theme throughout these pages and, frankly, throughout your career. Heck, after 18 years, I still work with this theme in my own business.

It's all about traction. Traction in real estate, your momentum, is dependent upon current clients, a pipeline of near and future clients, and ultimately, a consistently higher number of free referrals from past clients.

If you are new-ish to the business, your job is to work *only* on clients and traction; your broker works with you on contracts and process. For the new-ish agents, there is a slightly counter-intuitive dynamic about getting started…you need to be gaining traction before you really know what you're doing. There is a life lesson in this somewhere, but in real estate, if you wait to get started with your first client, if you wait until everything is perfect and you feel super prepared and your knowledge base is super ramped up, you'll be too late.

We call this the getting-ready-to-get-ready syndrome. You must get started fast. Your broker will/should help you with your first few clients—they better help you with your first few clients. Your job is to go get them quickly. More on this topic later.

If you are a seasoned or somewhat seasoned Realtor, then you already have the contracts and process down, and we're simply focusing on traction and an improved pipeline. Real estate school taught you the legalities—contracts, ethics, finance, etc. It taught you how to DEAL with business. School does not teach you how to FIND business. This program is all about consistently FINDING business.

> *You can only become truly accomplished at something you love. Don't make money your goal. Instead, pursue the things you love doing, and then do them so well that people can't take their eyes off you.*
>
> — Maya Angelou

I HEART REAL ESTATE

I heart real estate, homes, people, success, my bank account, being an entrepreneur. Pick one. This mindset parameter is a test of identifying what motivates you to be here, and assessing if that motivation is sustainable. What is the candy that is wooing you to real estate? You only need one solid motivation, one that a few bumps in the road, a challenging client or two, a learning curve, or an intense year of building a new business will not shake. Let's take a minute and identify your core motivation.

This is not a pass-fail test. Find the one or two that speak to you, that represent you at a deep level. Which of these apply to you?

- I love to talk houses with anyone who will listen.
- I attract people.
- I like to talk to people.
- I am generally a confident person.
- I stop in to open houses just to see how people live or decorate.
- I spend hours on real estate websites.
- I re-design houses when I'm in them. "Oh, you could move this wall, open up this room, add a window and a French door!"
- I like to win.
- I am financially motivated.
- I am known as a hard worker.
- I want to own my own business.

What is your motivation? While not a pass-fail test, the concept here is your commitment, your resolve. Are you really committed to making this career choice work? Over the years of working with agents getting their start, I have seen agents succeed at high levels while others get frustrated and fall out. As with any big endeavor, getting in touch with your core motivation can be the cornerstone to your success and your ability to stick with it.

And there may be people in your world who attempt to talk you out of your new career path. I ran into this. This is not necessarily a bad thing. If the people in your life can easily talk you out of something, then it's an indication that you are not yet clear and have not fully and convincingly presented your case and vision (you do not yet fully embrace it). Or it may be possible that the key people in your life lean negative or risk-averse. Perhaps they're well-meaning, but the risk factor of a 100% commission career may not rest well with someone in your life. Getting in touch with your resolve is foundational to any new chapter and will help you power through the naysayers.

LOOKING FOR ENCOURAGEMENT IN ALL THE WRONG PLACES

I spent years looking for encouragement, cheerleaders, a nod of approval, a sign, to jump into a real estate career. Perhaps your process was shorter than mine. Mine took years. Before I even looked at my first real estate license class, three different people talked me out of real estate as a career...a family friend, my first Realtor, and the biggest culprit, me.

The family friend was a 30+ year veteran of the industry. Her message was consistent, "It's harder than you think," and, in a parental sort of way, I think she wanted me to have some impressive corporate career.

My first Realtor, to whom I reached out to explore real estate as a career, talked me out of it. His position was more of the it's-harder-than-you-think, with a dose of stay-with-a-regular-paycheck-and-benefits.

And so I kept talking myself out of it. My cornerstone motivation, while developing, was not yet firmly in place. And so I kept talking myself out of it. I stayed in the corporate world well past my enjoyment of that scene.

And then, finally, years later, it was my friends who owned the small brokerage who enthusiastically said, "You would be great!" I had found my cheerleaders.

Because I had been laid off with a severance package and had a couple of contract gigs, a European travel stint, and the pleasure of living inexpensively, I was in a position to start my real estate career full-time. Let's take a closer look at part-time versus full-time.

FULL-TIME OR PART-TIME, YOU MUST KNOW YOUR CRAFT

For various personal and life reasons, some Realtors start out part-time. I get that. There are many very successful full-time Realtors out there who started part-time. For example, the stay-at-home parent who is shifting back into the professional world, or the investor Realtor who starts out with a few personal flip properties. Sometimes those agents really take off in year two or three. This book is written with the full-timer in mind, but applies to all Realtors whose heads are in the game. Part-timers, keep reading.

If you are starting out part-time or if you are initially dabbling in real estate to get a feel for whether it is a good fit for you, or perhaps if you got your license to work some personal real estate investments for you and your family, this book is designed to lay out the foundation of a full-time career and it may be exactly what you need. This book can serve as a tool to help you move toward full-time.

If you are part-time, make sure your knowledge base is full-time. What I mean by that last statement has everything to do with the NAR Code of Ethics and your responsibility to represent your client at a high level, to be their fiduciary. The body of knowledge we are responsible for in this business is enormous. Failure to study and pay attention like a full-time agent can seriously screw up a deal and put your client at risk.

When agents start part-time, I always like to help them identify a jumping-off point, the point at which they will go full-time. The jumping-off point tends to be one of two things; either a date on the calendar, or a certain amount of money in the bank. Or both. Such as, I will have $20,000 in the bank by January 1st, or my target is to resign May 31st.

So what would it take for you to go full-time? Is it January 1st? Is it the end of the school year? Is it the beginning of the school year, when the kids are finally back in school? Is it $10,000 in the bank? $30,000? Setting a target and writing it down helps tremendously. Write it down, set that benchmark in your brain, and start organizing your world around it. Tell your friends about your target. Send me a message online with your target (see links last chapter). And then send me another message when you hit it.

And what about insurance? This can be a tough one, a real reality check. If you or a family member has a serious medical issue, you need to fully understand your medical insurance options before venturing into self-employment. This alone keeps many people in employee mode. Understand this important detail and how it impacts you and your family before you jump from part-time to full-time.

GOING PRO

This book is best for the full-on, full-time agent. Part-timers (and brand new agents) will have more transactional, broker-type questions and fewer business-building questions. This book is about building a business. There is a big difference.

I train full-time Realtors to be good business professionals, to run businesses. I train Realtors to represent the Realtor community at a high level. I train Realtors to help them change their lives. I train Realtors to help them win raving fans and repeat clients. I train Realtors to increase the professional collective standards of what it means to be part of this community.

When agents are part-time, or hobbyists, they run the risk of not putting in the time it takes to know everything they should know. The volume of information real estate pros are held accountable for is staggering. As we have an obligation to our fellow professionals to uphold our industry, we have a substantially larger obligation to the public and the public trust to be consummate professionals. Realtors who take this lightly should consider handing in their license. I know that is a strong statement, but it is frustrating when you encounter a Realtor who doesn't know what they are doing. And more importantly, the client deserves a knowledgeable professional.

Anyone who takes this lightly is forgetting the Realtor Code of Ethics. For most people, a real estate transaction represents the largest financial transaction of their lives. I have often thought it should be much more difficult to get a real estate license. The enormity of what we do with a buyer or seller, the amount of money involved, the legality of that contract and that deed and that title, the estate, the investment, the financial plan, the life event—be it a marriage, a divorce, a new child, empty nesting, an estate, a move-up, a size-down—is hugely significant.

Now that we have reviewed the focus of the book and your foundation, let's get started with the task of building your business.

CHAPTER 6

It's a Race

What if the REALTOR® success quotient, the key to who stays in the business and who doesn't, was speed? What if the speed at which you gained your first ten clients had more to do with your longevity in the business, your likelihood to have a year two and three, than talent and intelligence? Not the strongest will survive, rather, the swiftest will have a sustainable real estate career?

What if speed was the number one indicator of a first-year Realtor's success? What if the key was simply who found clients quickly? And then more clients quickly? This is my argument…that the key to your success is gaining clients and a pipeline quickly. It is a bit of a race.

Like any race, you can train for it. Let's look at five specific race factors, and how you can best position yourself in that aspect of the race.

RACE FACTOR #1: YOUR PSYCHE

It's a race because of your psyche. Remember, I have trained hundreds of first-year agents with thousands of observations and conversations. And here is an important insight: Gaining a few clients quickly will do more for your psyche than the best self-help book out there.

How long did it take you to get your license? How long had you been thinking about it before you even took your license classes? How long did it take you to really decide to take this step toward a new profession? And how much money have you spent in that process? For most of you, it's been a while. At least months, and in some cases, years.

Your brain is ready.

Your brain has been working toward this for a long time. Your brain needs a client quickly. Psychologists will call this your reticular activating system, your RAS. Your RAS is a loose collection of neurons connected somehow to your brainstem. Your RAS is the general sleep regulator, and it is also directly related to how your brain processes information. Your RAS is in play when your brain is actively searching for the right information or experience to fill the gaps. It's the same thing as researching that blue Mini Cooper S convertible with the white stripe that you so desire, and all of a sudden seeing them everywhere around town. Your RAS was looking for them; your RAS was processing that information. (By the way, although you'll look cool, that Mini Cooper is a bit small to haul clients around on property tours.)

In your new or renewed real estate endeavor, your brain needs clients quickly, it needs to fill in the blanks. Without clients and client leads, your brain will have a tendency to fill in the gaps with noise, inner chatter that is not your ally. Your RAS will always work to fill in the gap, fill it in with anything somehow relevant.

If you are saying to yourself repeatedly, "ten clients, ten clients, ten clients", your brain becomes your advocate in making that happen. Same thing goes if your inner dialogue is "I'm not sure I like this." If you are thirty days in without a solid client lead or two or ten... let's just say it gets noisy in your head. I could make a list of a hundred agents who would give a nod of understanding to this noise concept. If you have been in the business for a bit, you may be nodding your head right now. Avoid the noise by getting your first ten clients as quickly as possible.

It's a race.

RACE FACTOR #2: SIXTY TO NINETY DAYS

It's a race because everything in this business, every paycheck, is sixty to ninety days out. And that is a fast client. For most people, having a paycheck every two weeks makes sense, and the only way this happens in real estate is to build a healthy pipeline of leads and clients.

The majority of leads that show up will benefit you, or materialize as a real client much further down the road—months down the road. It is definitely delayed gratification. Your cousin's friend who is probably moving to town next summer. The neighbor whose elderly mother is declining. The investor who intends to purchase two properties sometime this year. Your friends with two kids and one on the way, who are still in their starter home and have a long list of repairs before they're ready to put the house on the market. The family about to put two kids through the local university. The new construction that won't produce a commission check for ten months. The rental property where the lease expires next spring. Your PhD-candidate friends who will most likely be moving next year. This is the reality of a pipeline. If you can find a lead that is ready today, such as a for-sale-by-owner or a motivated and financially qualified and unrepresented open house guest, or your friend who calls and says, "OMG, I found the house I want to buy!", that is as good as it gets.

The ideal focus in your real estate business is the client lead who is ready in 30 to 60 days. That is a motivated and qualified short-term lead. Your pipeline will include short-term and long-term leads. It will also include motivated and not motivated leads, qualified and not qualified leads. Your pipeline will include leads that result in a client, and leads that were never really a lead in the first place.

So how does the pipeline concept line up with your financial cushion and the need for your next paycheck? Most of us have been used to a paycheck every two weeks. If your real estate paychecks are sixty to ninety days out, then how does that work for you? What are your monthly expenses? Are you tapping into your savings and, if so, for how long? It's definitely a race.

If you're one of the lucky ones whose financial cushion is not really an issue, you still need clients quickly because of the other race factors. If you're one of these "lucky" ones, beware, as you'll have a higher risk of getting caught up in the getting-ready-to-get-ready syndrome.

It's still a race.

RACE FACTOR #3: YOUR BANK ACCOUNT

It's a race because of your bank account. You can get varying opinions on this topic. Everyone talks about the financial cushion needed to get started. You have living expenses saved up, right?

Four-month financial cushion. Six-month cushion. Nine-month cushion. I lean toward the six-month cushion for getting started in real estate, and here's why. Two months' reserve can be gone in a nanosecond. Let's just agree that time flies and that you can get sucked into the learning and ramp-up portion of this business (which we are going to avoid…see getting-ready-to-get-ready section). Whatever your cushion, just subtract two months to make room for error. So if you have a six-month cushion, treat it like it's a four-month cushion, because two months can slip away easily, and it's sixty to ninety days out for any given client to turn into a paycheck. I think you get the picture. Assume that time will fly faster than you think.

It's a race.

RACE FACTOR #4: CONFIDENCE

It's a race because you'll gain skills and confidence faster by *doing*. You will gain infinitely more confidence faster by doing than you will in the classroom. Experience is the best teacher. I have heard of brokers who tell their new recruits, go get your first client then come see me. I prefer the brokers who train the recruits on how to find and engage and convert that first client, but the point is that the real learning and confidence building starts with a client in hand.

Don't wait until things are perfect and you're beginning to feel confident. John Maxwell speaks to this in his book *Failing Forward: Turning Mistakes Into Stepping Stones for Success.* He deftly challenges us to fail often, faster and better. Get out of prep mode and into ACTION. You WILL get better. Get out of your head and into action.

It's a race.

RACE FACTOR #5: NOTHING

It's a race because nothing leads to nothing. You may be fabulous with people, a great listener, an exceptional advocate, a twenty-year marketing professional, super smart, super detailed, organized, a market expert, a leader in your field, maybe you've been a mortgage professional or designer or builder for ten years. You're awesome, you've got game, you've got skills. Great.

Without a client, or three, or five, or ten, and a pipeline of potential clients, you have nothing. Nothing.

Can we agree that you intend to have a paycheck, earn commission, and be profitable? Right. It's a business. This is really simple… CLIENTS QUICKLY. It's a race. Treat it like a race. Get there faster than everyone else.

Now that we are clear on race day and urgency, let's explore some steps you can take to move in that direction immediately.

ACTION ITEM: EVERY DAY

"The main thing is to keep the main thing the main thing."
— Stephen Covey, *The 7 Habits of Highly Effective People*

In the introduction, I said this book is practical and actionable. The goal here, whether new or relaunching, is to gain traction quickly, and the ACTION ITEMS are designed to help you create that traction. The more you engage in the ACTION ITEMS throughout the book, the more traction you will have by the time you get to the last chapter.

Here is how critical this action thing is…it has everything to do with the cause and effect delay in the life cycle of real estate sales. All your habits today, the things you are doing, the conversations you are having, the schedule you are keeping, the shiny objects you are avoiding, will show up sixty to ninety days from now. So your ability to course-correct when you realize that next month is thin on or void of paychecks, is critical and has a delay.

In retail sales, or the restaurant business, you may be able to course-correct a lot faster by putting a big new banner outside or running a margarita special in August or a teacher special in September to get people through the door. That course-correction may be more like a speedboat revving its engines to make a solid push toward increased cash flow. The real estate sales cycle correction is more like turning a sailboat around. When you realize you need to get from point A to point B, it's a bit of a big, slow three-point turn to get there.

In your gaining traction progress, what you do today matters. Actually, what you did sixty to ninety days back matters most— what you do today matters next.

So let's get started.

EVERY…SINGLE…DAY, you must do something that has the likelihood of finding a client or client lead (or three, or five, or ten). Write that down!

Some of the ACTION ITEMS are directly related to the chapter subject, some not as much. What is important is the extent to which you are doing something every single day that has a strong likelihood of you gaining a client. Clients faster.

Remember *traction and clients quickly*. Embrace the 8:00 AM every day mantra of *traction and clients quickly*. Put a sticky note on your forehead, laptop, bathroom mirror, cell phone screen, somewhere that reminds you what your job is today. I have a bit of a daily mantra, practically tattooed on my wrist, that says: what is my fastest route to a solid client or paycheck today? It's how I start my day so I get the most important things done first.

A little guidance with the ACTION ITEMS…do not proceed to the next chapter until you have completed the ACTION ITEM in the current chapter. Let's just say it's a bit of a board game, and you do not get to proceed to the next level without completing that ACTION ITEM. No cheating. Trust me on this. Just do it.

WHAT TO SAY

Every chapter will include some scripts, what to say. Let's scuba dive into that topic for a minute.

When I first started in real estate, I rejected the concept of scripts. Even the word, script, was a bit of a four-letter-word thing for me. I was very clear that I never wanted to be that salesy-sounding type of Realtor. Being authentic was super important to me, and I was going to succeed in this business on my terms. I was not going to memorize the book of Realtor sales-pitchy things to say, I was just going to talk to people, I was going to be myself.

You may have some sort of corporate sales background. Or maybe you have experience in retail or a call center or a medical setting. And on day one of your new job, your boss or sales director placed a manual on your desk with the directive to memorize, quiz on Friday. You memorized what to say because in that environment, on that team, everyone said the same thing the same way. The team or the industry had figured out the most effective way to communicate and you were expected to be up to speed quickly. Failure to do so could cost you your job.

Here's what I did with the script manual when I first started in real estate...I ignored it. Or so I thought.

Someone had given me a set of CDs, I think it was *The Millionaire Real Estate Agent* book. And I started listening to these in my car. When I listen to non-fiction books in my car, I tend to listen in a somewhat passive manner, and the same CD or track or chapter or podcast will play two or three or four times in a row, sometimes over days or weeks, before I realize that I am on a merry-go-round with the material. I had been listening to these CDs over and over and over again. And a funny thing happened.

I was with clients and they threw some objection on the table. I do not even remember what the specific statement was...it would have been something like, "why should we hire you" or "we think we'll wait" or "we are interviewing other agents" or "will you reduce your commission." Again, I do not remember the actual question, but what I do remember is that some near perfect and poetic words came out of my mouth at the right time and I handled the objection like a pro. I remember almost being startled, like someone else was in my body delivering the poetic prose. It was a huge bump in my confidence and I knew, at that moment, that I had been practicing scripts. The words that came out of my mouth, without hesitation, in that moment of need, were directly from the CDs that had been on replay-replay-replay mode in my car. Without realizing it, I had been practicing scripts. At that point, I became more intentional with practicing what to say. I picked up the manual.

So let's get started with what to say.

ACTION ITEM: CALL YOUR MOTHER

Call your mother. Seriously, call your mother (or your sister or bff), and here's what you are going to say:

> *"Mom (sister, bff), I just started at [broker name] today! OMG, I am so excited! Wish I had done this earlier. I need your help. This is day one of the training program and the very first assignment they gave me was to call you! This business is seriously referral-based, and I have big goals. Will you help me? It's now my job to know the real estate needs of my friends and family and their friends and families, so there is a basic question, actually two questions, that I need to ask you. 1. Are you anticipating any real estate needs this year? 2. Is there anyone you know who may need my services this year? It's pretty much my job to ask this question, and who better to start with than you? I really super appreciate your support."*

We'll talk more about scripts throughout the book, but I need you to trust me on this call-your-mother (or the other people who love you) task. I have brand-new agents who get their first piece of business all the time because they called their mother and asked. If the actual wording of this script, or any script, does not really work for you, just tweak it…make it work, modify it to make it authentic. But do not skip.

This call-your-mother script is the basic lead generation question (or some form thereof) that you will be asking all the time. Write it out a few times. Stand up, walk around, and read it out loud a few times. Find your version of it. Own it, internalize it.

Keep calling your mother or your designated bff. Get these folks in your court. As soon as there is a glimpse of them supporting you at a high level, then send some flowers or a personal thank-you note or make them dinner or do something special. Get them in your court and keep them there. This is not a one-time phone call; this is an ongoing conversation. Call your mother.

CHAPTER 7

WHO IS THE BOSS OF ME?

YOU'RE YOUR OWN BOSS

You are a REALTOR®. The good news? You are your own boss. The bad news? You are your own boss. Don't be a lousy one.

You've worked for someone else before. Most of us have. You showed up on time, you got the most important things done every day, you planned out your vacations carefully, you figured out how to run your life and get important things done—buying groceries, taking kitty to the vet, driving kids to school early, meeting the repair guy, preparing for family visiting over the holidays. You figured out what to do when your child was sick. You made the most out of your weekends. You figured it out. You may have been tired, but you figured it out. For years, you figured it out. You were amazing with that forty to fifty-hour, or more, obligation every week. You had to… it meant job stability, it paid the bills.

Why would you treat your real estate business any differently? Why would you treat someone else's business with more respect and reliability than your own?

Once I really understood this concept, I started regularly asking myself these questions:

- Am I being a good boss?
- Was I a good boss today?
- If I was a lousy boss today, what got in my way?
- Am I doing the things I need to do today to build my pipeline?
- What is my fastest route to a new client or paycheck today?
- If I were to give myself a performance review for today or the past week or month, how would I rate?
- Would I hire me?
- Am I maintaining a full-time schedule?
- Do I look busy or did I actually gain traction this week?
- How many hours did I actually work this week?
- Did I do what I said I was going to do?
- Did I add to my pipeline today?

You are the CEO of you. Ask yourself, what can I do today to gain a lead? Do that first thing every day.

For a minute, let's pretend that I am your boss. What if I told you on your first day that, in order to keep your job, you have to sign one client per week and that is what everyone else at the brokerage did when they started? And you did not know any better, you took my word. Or two appointments and ten substantive real estate conversations every week? And that you had to turn in that report every Monday morning. And if the report was short, then you would be on a performance-improvement program, because I only wanted producers on the bus. So what if the golden rule for keeping your job was sign one client per week? Would you do it? This is simply an exercise in setting a daily or weekly performance standard or two for you, then making sure you hit it.

Be a good boss.

ACTION ITEM: THE FASTEST ROUTE TO YOUR NEXT CLIENT

Most of you are independent contractors, and by now you recognize that you are in the business of talking to people about real estate. No conversations, no clients. So let's start at the top.

The vast majority of agents have a referral-based business; the majority of their clients come from folks they already know, or that those folks know. Statistically, eight out of your first ten clients will come from someone you already know or someone they know. Those folks are most likely in your phone right now.

Let's explore some of the fastest routes to gaining a client.

ONE: Your Phone Is Power

The fastest route to gaining a client today is your phone, the contact list you already have, the people you already know.

Keep this super simple, do not overthink. Here are some options of what to say:

- I have an announcement, do you have a minute?
- I have a quick business question, do you have a minute?
- I have two questions, one personal, one business, do you have a minute?
- Did you see my Facebook post? Big announcement!
- Are you anticipating any real estate needs this year, or know of anyone who may be in need of my services?
- I want to add my name to the list of people you call when

you have a real estate question.

- I have big goals. I need your support.

And for the best people in your phone, the sort of folks on speed dial—if they are on speed dial—they deserve to hear your full story, your why, your passion. Tell your story. Engage them in your story and your motivation, your goals, your excitement.

Your job is to talk to people about real estate. What if your framework for every working day was to simply talk to ten people? See if they have any real estate needs, or know someone who does, or knows someone you should be talking to? How hard is that? Keep it simple and on task. You could walk the block, go to the park, the mall, your church, the kids' school, hold an open house. But the fastest route is your phone. You can crank out ten conversations in a minimal amount of time over the phone. In person may be more effective, but it's slower.

TWO: Do FSBOs Eat Their Young?

The next fastest route is the For Sale By Owners (FSBOs) and expired listings. Why? Because these folks are ready to sell today. (Check the professional standards in your area and with your brokerage before reaching out to FSBOs or expireds.) Right away, start stopping by and calling on FSBOs in your area. Here is what you say:

> *"I am Susan Realtor (you always have to disclose your credentials), I live in the area and saw your sign. I wanted to ask you a couple of questions, do you have a minute? Can you tell me a little about the house? What is the price? If I had a qualified buyer, are you prepared to pay a buyer agent commission? Are you considering hiring a Realtor? I'd like to come see the house real quick...can I swing by this afternoon?"*

One of my first clients came from an FSBO across the street from me. I was nervous. I did not know these people, but I knew the street. I called them. They wanted to give it a go for a couple of weeks. I stayed in touch. They got tired of the process and buyer no-shows. It became my first listing.

Industry research says that 80% of FSBOs will end up hiring a Realtor. So be a resource, build the relationships, and make these conversations a regular part of your business.

THREE: Open Houses Can Make A Million

We have top producers whose whole careers were built on nothing but open houses and stellar follow-up. Now they work by referral. Cool, eh? Open houses get you in front of buyers and neighbors. They put you in the role of Realtor super fast, and no one who walks through the door knows that you're new. The job with an open house is to first know about the house and neighborhood, make the listing agent look good to the seller, and gain leads. I know many successful agents who got their start cranking it out with open houses. This is an especially solid option if you are new to town or do not have much of a local sphere. Talk with your broker about open-house opportunities in your office.

We could write an entire chapter on talking to your friends and sphere (your phone contact list), an entire chapter on FSBOs, an entire chapter on open houses. You could easily spend an hour online on each of these topics. Your broker most likely has a class on each topic. We will build on these topics throughout the book. The task at this point is simple: get started with action in each of these right away, as they have a high likelihood of being your fastest route to your first ten clients.

Here is a recommended minimum schedule:

- Three open houses every month

- Ten conversations every day
- One FSBO outreach every day

Those are minimums. For agents who specialize in one area of the business, the schedule may look like this:

- The open house specialist will do an open house every day, six days a week.
- The phone pro will have 20 real estate conversations every day.
- The FSBO specialist will have a goal to have an appointment with an FSBO every day.

ACTION ITEM: IDENTIFYING YOUR TOP 100

Get out your phone. Get your neighborhood list. Your church directory. Your Christmas card list. Your kids' school directory. Your former colleagues. Your golf league. Don't forget your family. In town or out of town or out of state…all of them. Your college friends. I have brand-new agents who got their first or second client because they called their cousin or college friend halfway across the country. You know a LOT of people! Let's identify your top 100, because I promise you, there is business in there. Your immediate job is to cultivate and coax the leads out of that top 100 list.

Who are your besties? If you had a party, they would be on the list. You follow these folks on Facebook. They know you. Get super clear on who your TOP 100 are, and get them on the phone. The faster you have a meaningful conversation with them about your new business, the faster you'll gain their trust and their referrals. And they want to help you. They love you and want you to succeed.

Ask for their support. Tell them you intend to earn their referrals. Ask if they anticipate any real estate needs this year. Who do they call when they have a real estate question?

When I started my real estate business in 1999, I threw a little party. When there is a new store or restaurant in town, they have a grand opening event, right? I figured I should do the same for my new business.

At the time, I rented this lovely little basement apartment in the woods on Shoal Creek in central Austin. I had just sold my house in north Austin and this was my interim landing place. It was serene, with an amazing patio in the woods. It was a nicely situated gathering place.

I knew I needed to engage my sphere to launch my real estate career. I invited my top 40 friends to my home for a happy hour (the landlord, owner, and upstairs occupant was on the list). I stopped the party in the middle, announced my new business, told them why I was excited about real estate, asked them for their support, gave them all my new business card, threatened to not let anyone go home without a referral, told them I was going to send them all an e-mail with my current contact information, told them I intended to earn their referrals, told them I loved them all, toasted to new beginnings, then got on with the party. The whole speech and toast took five minutes. That party and my post-party outreach (the email and a personal call thanking them for coming) jumpstarted my career. Six of my first ten clients came directly or indirectly from that party outreach.

ACTION ITEM: TOP 100, WHAT TO SAY WHEN YOU CALL

Remember that I told you in the introduction that this book was actionable? And that your results, your ability to gain traction, will be directly related to your ability to tackle the action? Start paying very close attention to getting the ACTION ITEMS done in each chapter. Put your foot on the gas pedal, don't let up, and crank out these calls, these conversations. You want a raise in real estate? You give yourself a raise by having more conversations.

So today's ACTION ITEM is this: Call one to twenty of your TOP 100, and here's what to say:

> *"Hey, Sam, it's [me]. Do you have a minute? I know you're at work, so I'll be fast. I wanted to let you know what I'm doing. I've thought about this for years, finally pulled the trigger, and I am now an associate with xyz Realty. Love it, wish I had done this sooner! So a couple of quick questions: 1. Do you have a go-to Realtor when you have a real estate question? [NO: Great, you do now! Or YES: Great, happy to be the second person on your list.] Second question: Are you anticipating any real estate needs this year or know anyone who may need my services? I appreciate you keeping me in mind. I'll send you an e-mail right away so you have my contact info. Everything good with you? Would love to do lunch or happy hour sometime, catch up. What's your schedule like the next couple of weeks?"*

CHAPTER 8

GOT CONFIDENCE?

CONFIDENCE

Your confidence—it is one of my favorite topics for new REALTORS®. Let's take a quick inventory on how you're showing up in the world.

How's your energy level? Do you like talking to people? When your learning curve is steep, do you keep your energy up, do you lean in? Do you exude confidence, or do you just muster it up? I call this your POWER SCORE.

POWER SCORE BASIC PREMISE

Why do some agents succeed while other well-intentioned agents never really make it? In five intense and insanely rewarding years of training new agents, I realized there is this somewhat intangible, yet moderately palpable thing that combines your energy, your confidence, your eye contact, your voice, your posture, your motivation, your nutrition, your internal dialogue…simply, how you're showing up in the world. We'll call this your power score.

Power score is not an introvert / extrovert thing. I know strong and confident introverts. I know extroverts who are negative, or a bit manic, or on the depression scale.

Because real estate is a people business, dependent upon attracting opportunity and having effective conversations, how you're showing up in the world—your personal ecosystem—is a foundational piece of your success formula. There is a reason we cover this early in the book, early in the process of your start or restart in the business. You could go through every ACTION ITEM in the book, not skip one, possibly complete everything faster than everyone else, but if your power score consistently dips into the low zone, you'll have trouble gaining clients and traction.

So here is a little task for you today: rate yourself on your power score. How are you showing up? This really is an ongoing activity and is rarely a straight line, rather more a process of ongoing course corrections. It's life, right? Tweaking what is working and what is not. Again, you are starting (or re-starting) a new chapter in your life, and we are addressing your foundation. Remember my sabbatical? I was addressing my foundation. My sabbatical was a solid course correction.

Be true with this exercise, be true with yourself, as you may have blinders on in some area of your life. I certainly have had my phases of denying something, or a delayed dealing with things, delayed course corrections. To remove the blinders, you may want to have this conversation with a trusted friend or two…how am I showing up? Narcissists typically do not know they are narcissistic, depressives may be in denial of how that is showing up in their lives, egotists are likely unaware of their self-absorption, the unhealthy may avoid the doctor. A good friend (or in some cases a skilled therapist) can help remove the blinders. I have heard the stories of many successful agents who first had to put their lives together in order for their businesses to materialize.

So how *are* you showing up?

POWER SCORE 1-3: THE LOW ZONE

You're having a hard time showing up with confidence and energy.

You are uncomfortable asking direct questions. When making business phone calls, you have a bit of a knot in your stomach. Perhaps you do not feel well. Your immediate circle leans negative and pessimistic and consistently attempts to sabotage your drive and optimism. Motivation is elusive, eye contact inconsistent, diet sucks, optimism a distant cousin. Obviously, this is not a good camp site.

If this is situational, then you may need to embrace the "fake it till you make it" mantra. If you're in a funk, find your funk reduction tools and push through it. If this is an ongoing pattern, talk with some valuable people in your life STAT and push this into the medium range ASAP.

Here's the deal: low power score, and you will have a hard time attracting clients or gaining rapport or trust. Address this ASAP.

POWER SCORE 4-6: THE MEDIUM ZONE

Medium can be situational. Maybe there are challenges at home and you have to muster up your energy and decide every day to bring your best self.

Medium can also be that nice and steady person of few words, the keen observer who is rarely the outspoken cheerleader but rather the reliable and consistent authority. Never the loudest voice in the room, medium can be the steady team player everyone relies on to get things done, often with little to no credit. Be careful about rating yourself medium when really you are a strong introvert. Remember, power score is not an introvert-extrovert thing. Rather, it is an indication of the extent to which you are attracting people.

Medium indicates that high is possible. If you are hanging out in the medium zone, pick one thing you can focus on this week that may bump your score up a point or two…incremental changes and tweaks. For example, this week I am going to call my two most positive friends, because I always feel so much better after we talk.

Or this week, I am going to start each day off with a good breakfast and a walk. Or this week, I am going to attend the neighborhood meeting, like I said I would. Or Sunday, I am going to clean my desk, because the clutter is messing up my brain. Hey, you started a new really big chapter in your life…sometimes confidence is a bit elusive in times of something big and new, so figure out what you need to tweak and make it happen.

POWER SCORE 7-10: THE HIGH ZONE

You rock the room, you attract people, you raise your hand often, you are consistently engaging. Most days, your energy is solid. You are your own best advocate. If you are an introvert (yes, introverts can have a high power score), you are attentive and articulate, a leader. You move quickly. If you hit a bump, you keep moving forward. You are willing to try things, you are positive and optimistic. You are consistently giving yourself that internal nod of approval. Swagger comes easy. You most likely have decent sleep, eating, and exercise habits. Obviously, high power score is good; it's where you want to hang out. Hanging out in the high power zone is key to attracting people and converting opportunity into actual clients.

Take a moment to identify two or three things that help you stay in this zone. This will be different for everyone. For me, my stay-in-high-power-zone formula is hugely dependent upon my sleep habits (I am a lifelong member of the eight-hour club), breakfast with protein (we have chickens), exercise (gardening, swimming, cycling), affirmations, loose-end management, and helping other agents. Like a compound pharmacy, it is my customized prescription. What is your prescription? What keeps you in the zone and, contrarily, what compromises your zone, your power score?

POWER SCORE AGILITY

We all have things that can throw us off our game. A big culprit for me is when there is too much on my plate, and then I get busy-head, and then my self-talk gets messy, and then I misplace my A+ confidence. I get frustrated, my compass is off, my grounding messed up. Being aware of those things doesn't necessarily mean we avoid them or order a second margarita; it often means we can course-correct faster. I know this impacts business, but I swear that power score agility may be the secret of life: your ability to course correct and adjust. Life, success, happiness, it's never a straight line, it's a bit of a moving target.

Drop perfection, embrace agility. What a relief when we can finally embrace this concept and give ourselves a break, relax a little, and simply course-correct! And then course-correct again, and again and again. This is what agility is. Your mindset, your energy, your production, your self-talk, your habits, your diet, your exercise program…it's never a straight line.

Your power score can change from day to day. This would be normal. What we are looking for is awareness, consistency, and your ability to course-correct faster. Let's call this power score agility. To show up solid in your business (heck, in your life), you need to consistently land in the medium-to-high range. Too much low and you'll be out of the business before you know it. Hang out in the high range, and you'll gain traction faster than everyone else.

Your power score is all about success from the inside out. Starting with you, your thoughts, your internal compass, how you're showing up. Your energy walks in the room before you do. Your swagger speaks louder than your words. How you think matters. While this is not a new concept, it is a foundational piece of your success formula.

Let's shift gears for a bit.

In the ACTION ITEM for this chapter, we are going to tackle a very specific topic all Realtors need to understand, and your comfort around the topic will make you look and feel smart. The topic is the affordability factor and how that ties into talking with renters, helping them get in the market and begin building equity.

ACTION ITEM: AFFORDABILITY FACTOR

First, the Lesson

In this activity, we're going to talk to friends who rent: anyone who rents. You may find yourself running seminars for first-time buyers, in which case this topic will come in handy. You could run a seminar for MBA students at the local university. First, let's review the math around what economists call the affordability factor.

Find a mortgage calculator online (in your google search bar, type in "mortgage calculator" and then just use the easy one on the screen). Hint: get a mortgage calculator app on your smartphone ASAP (there are many to choose from).

EXAMPLE 1 - Do this math:

Year 1992 - $150,000 mortgage x 8.5% interest rate = $1,153 payment (principal and interest)

Year 2016 - $240,000 mortgage x 4.0% interest rate = $1,145 payment (principal and interest)

Your payment on a $240,000 mortgage in 2016 is the same as it was on a $150,000 mortgage in 1992.

In its most basic form, this is the affordability factor.

EXAMPLE 2

Here is another example that is particularly helpful in explaining to a renter, especially in a market that is appreciating, why waiting for a year to buy a home can be very expensive.

The home at 123 Southside Drive is currently on the market in the Shady Grove neighborhood, a very popular and trendy area of town. We are currently seeing multiple offers in this area of town, so let's say it sold for full price and the buyer obtained a mortgage at the current market rate of 4% with 20% down. Here is how the payment plays out:

$225,000 price
$180,000 loan
4% interest rate
$859 payment (principal & interest)

Now let's look at buying this exact same home one year later... let's say prices are going up in Shady Grove (you have seen the trends), and this exact same home one year later may be selling for $240,000 and interest rates will go up (they will go up—economic fact). Let's say interest is at 5% a year from now. Here is how this plays out:

$240,000 price
$192,000 loan
5% interest rate
$1,031 payment (principal & interest)

Same house one year later costs $172 more per month to own. That is over $2,000 a year. And what if $225,000 is the maximum price this particular first-time buyer is approved for based on his income, debt, and credit score? That buyer, if he waits one year, may not be able to afford Shady Grove. He may be pushed out a little further toward the suburbs because he has been priced out of Shady Grove.

This is the affordability factor.

Now let's get some mileage out of your understanding of this topic. Here's a tip: write a quick blog article on the topic. Use a real example in your area with current pricing and interest rates, and get this information out to people you know. When you blog, you can tweet it, Facebook it, Instagram it, and e-mail it to get mileage.

Blogging also starts building your credentials among your sphere that you really know what you are talking about.

While we're on the blog topic, a quick side note. Blog articles help people find you online, especially for obscure topics. Truth is, as I type this, I received a call yesterday from a woman in central Austin who had found a 2010 blog article I wrote about flight paths in Austin. It was a simple little article I wrote about my Northwest Hills home (direct flight path), with commentary on the neighborhoods in Austin where the planes were quite low over the neighborhoods. I have another article out there somewhere in the googlesphere about plumbing static tests and the lovely process of jackhammering a slab to address old crumbling pipes (I've been there, twice, and survived). I get at least one phone call a year from someone, all over the country, who wants to talk static tests. I always call them back. I like to help; it earns me nice person points, and boosts my power score.

So how can we engage people on this affordability factor topic?

You're talking to renters. Quickly, make a list of everyone you know who rents, or probably has a lot of friends or colleagues who rent. If there is an employer in your town that hires a lot of millennials, figure out who you know who works there. I am in Austin, Texas, so this topic is a great tool for my 20-something and 30-something friends who work at tech start-ups downtown, or who work at Google, or Facebook, or Apple.

One way or another, figure out how to have this conversation with as many renters as possible:

> *"Oh, you're renting? Have you thought about buying? You know, interest rates are historically low. Like, they'll never be lower. They will go up . . . not if, but when. Well, I thought of you this morning because I was thinking of this. Have you thought of*

buying? If you did buy, what neighborhood interests you?"

"Your timing can be critical because when interest rates go up, let's say from 4% to 5%, that will impact how much home you could buy. If you qualified for that cute $250,000 home in Shady Grove today, you may only qualify for a $230,000 home next year. And prices are going up. I'd hate to see you miss the market, miss the opportunity to live in Shady Grove. Does this topic interest you? I thought so. Would you like to meet for coffee to talk about it more, or I can introduce you to a mortgage broker just to explore your options . . . which sounds better? Is there anyone else you know who is renting who should probably take a look at this?"

"Hey, while we're on the topic, is there anyone you know who may need my services this year? We're already setting up appointments for this summer. Keep me in mind . . . I'd love the opportunity to help your friends and colleagues. I'm going to shoot you an e-mail real quick so you have my info handy."

Here's a bonus tip:

Is there a company in town that likes to run lunch-and-learns for their employees? Lots of companies do this. So if you have a friend who works for IBM, or xyz corporation, or a communal work space, ask them if you can do a thirty-minute lunch-and-learn about why now is a good time to buy or invest in real estate. These opportunities typically involve you providing lunch. You could share the lunch-and-learn with a lender. Think outside the box in order to get in front of your target audience.

CHAPTER 9

OMG! I Have To Talk To People?

CONVERSATIONS

Chit chat is ok. Socializing is ok. But to talk on purpose for business? THIS is how it works: you have to ask for business. Falling short of actually asking for business will seriously impact your bank account.

In the last chapter, we addressed your power score and how you talk to yourself. In this chapter and the next (and a couple more after that), we dig into the practicalities and specifics of talking to people about real estate. You can talk to yourself all day long, but the last I checked, unless you are personally buying twenty properties this year, your internal dialogue does not directly lead to new client opportunities.

You're in the business of talking to people about real estate. Wrap your brain around that.

You may be amazing online at capturing leads via various techy strategies, but you still need to *talk* to those people. The goal with any online lead, any lead, is to get them on the phone. Sometimes the script is simply "What's your phone number?" Keep this principle in mind: take your online leads offline, and your offline leads online.

The fastest route to rapport and, ideally, an appointment is an actual conversation. If you have an online lead and all of your communication is electronic, there will be a greater chance of that person disappearing, no-showing, or simply not responding. In sales and in real estate, keep this principle close at hand: the person who talks to the most people will have the most opportunities and will make the most money.

And again, you do not have to be an extrovert to make it in this business. It helps a lot, but it is not a rule. If you lean shy or lean introvert, this is a critical point. I know one of the top REALTORS® in the country (he now coaches top agents in the country), and have actually heard him say on stage something about not really being a people person. He prefers solitude over crowds. But what he realized very quickly when he first got started thirty years ago was that he liked going to the bank. And he made peace, quickly, with the concept that he was in the business of having conversations with people about real estate.

The consistent number and quality of your real estate conversations is everything, the cornerstone of your success. I believe this so strongly that when I talk about making a certain number of contacts per day, you do not get to count voicemail messages left, text messages, e-mails, or Facebook exchanges. While those touches add up and will be a solid piece of your overall strategy to connect, do not confuse online and text interactions with actual conversations.

ACTION ITEM: MONDAYS!

Mondays are big follow-up days for Realtors. And any other day for that matter. Get out your calendar right now, plug in a repeating weekly appointment for every Monday from 9:00 to 11:00 AM, and call it FOLLOW-UP MONDAY. This is the day every week where you follow up with anyone with whom you have recently had a real estate conversation. This timeslot will be a catch-all for any loose ends, anyone you meant to call back but for some reason or another has not yet happened. Follow-up Monday is a safety net. When I implemented this in my business, I greatly reduced the likelihood of waking up in the middle of the night realizing I had forgotten to follow up with someone. I have also implemented a calendar reminder for 8 AM every day that pops up and tells me "lead follow-up." This anchors my daily schedule and is priority #1 every day.

Speaking of follow-up, you need a good system. You need a good CRM, Customer Relationship Management. There are many to choose from. Your broker may provide one, your local board or MLS may provide one. Prices range from free to inexpensive to really expensive. CRM choice is a big discussion among agents who are always looking for the right tools to help them run their businesses.

Personally, I do not care if you start off with a shoebox and index cards. Or a notebook or a spreadsheet. If those work for you, then great. For now. You will want to graduate to an online system, but for now, use what works for you. And a little warning on the shoebox index card approach—if you lose that box, you just lost the greatest asset in your business, so an online tool makes a tremendous amount of sense.

Commit now to being an amazing follow-up person. Consider follow-up director as the second item in your job description. First item, generate leads; second item, follow up. Adopt this mantra, these affirmations, right now: I am the most ridiculously amazing and super consistent follow-up person ever. I am a follow-up super star. My follow-up skills and consistency make me a lot of money.

Here's what to say to anyone with whom you've had a real estate conversation over the past few days or on the weekend:

"As I said I would, I just wanted to follow up on our real estate conversation from Saturday. Is this an OK time? Great. So tell me again

what you're thinking, what your needs are. [Listen. Ask questions.]" Then set a timeframe for your next follow-up and e-mail something of value [maybe just a follow-up e-mail to recap the conversation or possibly an article on the topic or a personal note]. Make a note in your calendar [or whatever system you're using, your CRM] for the follow-up.

Then ask this question (the POWER QUESTION which we will scuba dive into in the next chapter): "Hey, real quick, while we're on the topic . . . Is there anyone else you know who may need my services this year? We're already setting up appointments for [summer] and I always want to make sure I am saving spots for my friends and their friends. Thank you for thinking about it. My business is primarily referral-based and I appreciate your support."

Yes, tweak as necessary. Always tweak the scripts so it sounds and feels natural for you.

ACTION ITEM: GET TO KNOW YOUR CLIENT RELATIONSHIP MANAGEMENT (CRM) SOFTWARE

This ACTION ITEM is simple: take 30 minutes and do a google search for best Realtor CRMs. Read a couple reviews comparing them. Maybe ask your Realtor network what CRM they are using and what they like best about it. The other option is take 30 minutes and go over a couple tutorials or best-practices articles on the CRM you are already using, or has been made available to you. The best CRM for you is going to be the one you actually use. So although your broker or board may provide one, if it is less than stellar or you are simply not using it because it is clunky or it is not intuitive or it is doo-doo, then either get better at it or find one that works for you. Your CRM, and using it, is very important to your success.

CHAPTER 10

WHAT TO SAY... AND HOW... AND WHY

POWER QUESTIONS

By now you understand that you are in the business of talking to people about real estate. Yes, this is a repetitive message throughout the book. But what do you say? Notice the subtitle does not say power *conversations* or power *presentations*. While those have their place, this is about power *questions*. When you realize that the majority of effective communication in this business (and in life, marriage, parenting, leading, and being a good friend) is simply asking good questions versus you doing all the talking and sounding amazing, brilliant, and experienced, it takes a lot of the pressure off and begins to put you in control of the conversation. It also puts you on the rapport fast-track. Just ask *questions, powerful* questions. Some questions are more strategic, more effective, than others. Let's scuba dive into this topic.

Being a question pro is a handy tool for so many situations—a handy tool for life, and a particularly handy tool with children, teenagers, and spouses. Ask more questions. Are they teaching this in schools these days? They should. It's a skill that makes everything work better. Asking good questions and having the patience to listen to the answers is the great ego-moderator skill.

Once you get the hang of this, not just professionally but even more importantly personally, it becomes part of your natural style. Notice the people in your life that you love to be around, that make you feel good, that always seem to get you talking, talking about your day, your experience, your opinion, your story, your challenges. They get you. The people that are really good listeners. I bet those feel-good skilled-listener people in your world consistently ask a lot of questions; it's how they operate. Start observing this. Also notice the style of people you know who are successful in some sort of sales or leadership. Notice their style of communication. I bet they are asking a lot of questions.

On the converse, the folks who annoy you, that you don't really care to be around or that wear on you or that you simply tune out, they're never asking questions. It's all about them, it's a lopsided conversation all the time. It's annoying and really limiting in sales and people businesses.

The 3 Question Rule

Experiment with this a bit. Without telling anyone what you are doing or allowing them to read this chapter, try it out on your kids, your spouse, the grocery store check-out clerk. Before you can say anything about yourself, your day, or your opinion, you have to ask three questions. You do not have a green light to talk (and in some cases talk, talk, talk, talk, talk...we'll address that somewhat annoying behavior later), until you have asked three questions.

The grocery store clerk says, "How are you?" You say, "I'm good. How are you?" (question #1). Listen to answer. "How long have you worked here?" (question #2). Listen to answer. "You're always so pleasant and I appreciate that. What do you like best about working here?" (question #3). Listen to answer. They'll remember you. If I ran a retail store, I would totally train the three question rule into my customer-facing team. I would make it a standard of how we operate.

The teenager. That's another book. I don't have kids. Try it. And then keep trying it. Do not tell them what you are doing. If the teen response is "I don't know," then with a smile try "Well, if you did know, what would it be?" Keep it up…it may drive them crazy but they'll eventually come along. Ultimately, they may start using it on you, or you'll observe them using it on their friends. It will be a very good day when you overhear your teen actually say to one of their teen friends, "Well, if you did know, what would it be?"

The spouse. I have one of those. Start trying the three-question approach on your beloved. When your spouse or significant other says something along the lines of "Whew, what a day," your typical response might be "I know! I was up at 5:30, I felt rushed all day, traffic was rough, and you know that meeting I told you about? Well, let me tell you what happened." Uh, no. You do not get to talk about your day until you have asked Mr. or Mrs. or bff three questions about "Whew, what a day!" Seriously, this three-question red light/ green light can transform a stalled or stuck or flat relationship. Eventually, tell your spouse or significant other about your three-question experiment and the two of you can start working on this approach together. We have done this in my household. It's not a perfect record and sometimes we joke about it…"Hey, you only asked me one question. I need my three on this topic." It's a bit of a game changer.

How does this apply in business? In the last chapter, we addressed your power score. Now in this chapter, we are going to talk about the power questions, what they are, and what they can do for your business success. The power questions are a supply of conversation-yielding go-to REALTOR® questions that will be the core of how you engage folks in effective real estate conversations. Tweak these to make them authentic to you and your style.

Here is POWER QUESTION set #1 (we'll call these PQs):

PQ #1: I wouldn't be doing my job

> "Hey, real quick . . . I wouldn't be doing
> my job if I didn't ask you this question.
> Is there anyone you know who may need my
> services this year? I appreciate you keeping

*me in mind. I'll send you a quick e-mail with
my contact information. Are you anticipating
any real estate needs this year?"*

PQ #2: Earn your referrals

*"I know you know a number of Realtors. I
just want you to know that it is my goal to
earn your referrals. Just planting the seed.
So what's the most important thing that you
value in a Realtor? While we're on the topic,
are you guys anticipating any real estate
needs this year?"*

PQ #3: The second on your list

*"I respect that you know another Realtor [or
that your sister is a Realtor or that you
like your old Realtor]. I'd love to be the
second on your list. Not everyone is the
right match, so keep me in mind. While we're
on the topic, are you anticipating any real
estate needs this year?"*

PQ #4: The only property?

*"Is this the only home you have to sell, or
are there others?"*

PQ #5: Who do you know?

*"Who do you know who may need my services this
year? We are already setting appointments
for fall."*

PQ #6: Mentioned real estate?

*"Is there anyone you know who has recently
mentioned real estate?"*

PQ #7: Who do you call?

*"Who do you call when you have a real estate
question?"*

You need to find yourself asking the power questions as often as possible. Get super comfortable with this. The more you ask these, the more comfortable, natural, and effective you will be. Start counting how many times you asked one of the power questions every day. It's your job. You could treat this like a game. The person asking these questions the most, without being annoying, wins.

Pretend that you are the national sales manager of your real estate business (because you are). What does a sales manager do? Sales managers set the sales targets for their team or division, establish a structure to support those goals, and then hold their team accountable for hitting those targets. Right? So what is your target? How many buyers and sellers do you need to help this year in order to hit your financial goals? Simple business plan, right? So as the national sales manager of your real estate business, shouldn't you know if your team is doing the work? You are the team. Keep a tally. Set a target.

Let's apply this concept to one of the top Realtors in the country... actually, let's clarify...one of the top under-30 Realtors in the country, Tim Heyl in Austin, TX. He made this very simple when he first started in real estate fresh out of college. He called his client leads "nurtures." Every day, five days a week, he started his day talking to people about real estate. He would not allow himself to consider it a day worked until he had identified five nurtures that day. That means he was adding twenty-five leads to his pipeline every week. Not all of them quality leads, but he was feeding his pipeline. And then he knew his math...five nurtures usually equaled one appointment. He was being a very good national sales manager of his real estate business.

HOW'S THE MARKET?

The how's-the-market question is foundational. Your mastery of this question is critical. Every day, you must have a really good answer to this question. And you should be getting this question every day. If you are not getting this question every day, then you are not having enough real estate conversations.

You should be getting this question every place you show up. You should be getting it at church, at the kids' soccer games, at the gas station, grocery store, neighborhood picnic, family dinners, open houses. Everywhere, every day. If you are not getting this question all the time, then no one knows you're in real estate. This is hands-down the most common and popular question and conversation-starter. So how is your market?

As quickly as possible, you need to become a subject matter expert on this topic. It's your job to get on top of this and stay on top of this. Pay attention, study, read, talk to other Realtors, talk to lenders, engage your friends on the topic, watch stats daily or weekly in your MLS. You could get in the habit of posting something to social media every single Monday with a how's-the-market commentary (tip: post it early morning, noon, or early evening when everyone is paying attention, not in the middle of the day when they're working).

So what do you say? There are two categories of approaches to this topic. One is the subject matter expert where, for example, you may write a blog article or do a quick video online talking about the market and some of its statistical dynamics. Have pertinent facts ready to go. The more facts, the better you sound. The other approach is the engage-the-consumer approach. Let's take a closer look.

Stats & Market Dynamics

Here are some common stats to monitor and work into your conversations:

> Inventory: *"Wow, there are 56 homes on the market in Shady Grove and about 20 are selling per month. That means on average it will take 2-3 months to sell. So here is what is selling…"*

> Inventory: *"Last month there were 80 homes for sale in the area, today there are 93. Don't miss the market. Who do you know who is thinking of selling?"*

Price trends: *"The average home price in Bay City went up 7% over this same time last year. This is influenced by our strong economy, low inventory, and all the new construction in the area. It may be a good time to sell. Let's chat."*

Interest rates: *"Interest rates bumped a tad recently and the Fed is indicating another bump early next year (hint: you need to study this). Even a quarter or half-point bump can seriously impact your monthly payment. Don't miss the market. Who do you know who is thinking of buying and would benefit from a decent strategy conversation?"*

Engage The Consumer

Here are some handy engage-the-consumer responses to the popular how's-the-market question. (Notice that there is a question on the end of each response.)

"The market? It's crazy awesome . . . why do you ask?"

"The market? It's great. Have you thought of selling?"

"Is it a good time to sell? It is for a lot of people, not so much for others . . . depends. What's up? What is your situation?"

"How's real estate? It's amazing! Wish I had done this years ago! You guys still live downtown?"

"Home sales are up x percent from this same time last year, and prices are up x percent in our neighborhood. That's solid. How long have you guys been in your home? Are you considering selling or know anyone wanting to move into this area?"

"The market? It amazes me. You know, with interest rates as low as they are, a mortgage payment on a $220k home today is about the same as a mortgage payment on a $120k home in 1995. It's called the affordability factor. The folks out there that are still renting need to take a serious look at that. What's your e-mail? I have a blog article on the topic I want you to see. When are you going to buy?"

ACTION ITEM: POWER QUESTIONS, DO IT!

Read the PQs again and the how's-the-market responses above out loud, ten times fast. You probably want to be by yourself when you do this. Another option is to pair up with another agent and plow through this exercise together. The goal of this quick exercise is simply speed and repetition. Speed and repetition. In fact, you may want to do this simple exercise every day this week and next week and the week after. Go over and over and over and over these questions. Speak them out loud, write them out on a notepad, type them out, record yourself on your phone and listen to them in your car (hands-free, of course). Speed and repetition.

The call:

Pick one of the PQs in this chapter and call someone, call five, call twenty…heck, walk your block and ask your neighbors. This is not an e-mail, it is not a post on Facebook. You must have conversations with people. Do not move on to the next chapter without this ACTION ITEM checked off.

So, for example, you would call ten friends and ask them real quick:

"Who do you know who may need my services this year? We are already setting appointments for fall."

How Are You Doing?

How are you showing up on the ACTION ITEMS? We are ten chapters into the book and your success will be directly related to your action versus time spent reading. Think of this paragraph as the teacher that you love checking on your homework progress. Remember your most favorite, kind teacher or professor you ever had? When Mrs. Favorite or Professor Kind genuinely checked in on your progress, that was a good thing. Right? They cared. I care. Consider this a nudge.

Remember the 10-20% that succeed according to industry stats? I think the 20% are the ones doing the *right* work. Every day, the 20% do something that has a high likelihood of creating a client quickly. We are all busy, I'm busy, you're busy, but is it the *right* busy? What if most of your activity is social media yet there are very few actual conversations? You are in the business of having meaningful conversations about real estate.

I know, you may be working your tail off. You may be cranking out open houses, taking as many broker classes as you can fit in, preparing awesome newsletters to send to your friends and neighbors, working on your buyer packets, spending hours on your social media profiles and campaigns. All of that matters. And none of that matters without conversations.

I see this all the time. And every broker and trainer in the country would say the same thing...busy with the wrong things.

Here's the good news: You can join the 20% by doing the right things with consistency. Every day, you have an opportunity to start or restart this pattern. Simply start building consistency with the things that matter the most. Do the things that matter most first. Every day. You can do this.

Again, this book works best if you're doing the action. Maybe you're reading the book through quickly first, then you're going to circle around and read it again doing the actual work. I get it. I scan material all the time. My point is this: if you're not doing the work of consistently having real estate conversations, you'll be at risk. If you delay, you may be at risk. If you are two weeks in or two months in and are still getting ready to get ready, you'll be at risk. I coached a Rookie of the Year where she had six clients lined up the day she got her license. She had been talking to everyone she knew for months, doing a countdown to Realtor license day.

Here's the deal. On any given day, your actions could be high action, or they could be low action. We all experience this. I experience this. On any given day, I may be totally in the game, and on another day, not even close—or worse yet, in denial that I *was* in the game when I was actually on the sidelines feeling busy. No one has efficiency immunity; it comes and goes. It is an ongoing process of being more and more accountable, more and more in the game.

Simply take inventory every day. How did I do today? Was I on the sidelines or was I on the field? How many conversations did I have today? Did I add anyone to my pipeline today? If you track your number of conversations, track the health of your pipeline, or somehow rate yourself each day, your patterns will show up, and this awareness is so incredibly valuable. Pay attention. Keep improving week after week. Were you off track on Monday? Fix it on Tuesday. Did you have an off week? It happens. Let go of perfection and embrace improvement. What course correction do you need to make next week?

CHAPTER 11

DOES PRACTICE REALLY MAKE PERFECT?

I felt a cleaving in my mind
* As if my brain had split;*
I tried to match it, seam by seam,
* But could not make them fit.*

The thought behind I strove to join
* Unto the thought before,*
But sequence ravelled out of reach
* Like balls upon a floor.*

— Emily Dickinson - I felt a cleaving in my mind

How often do you find yourself assessing what you said, or did not say, in the rearview mirror? If only I had said this or that. How often was there a missed opportunity for brilliance or gentleness or connectivity or a perfectly timed power punch or the perfect close? Or the times you simply forgot to ask the right, if any, power question, or stumbled over an objection? Let's take a closer look at building muscle memory on what to say.

TIME ON TASK OVER TIME

In your new REALTOR® gig, you need to move toward expertise status swiftly and systematically. For those of you relaunching, you may need to brush up on your knowledge base and skills.

What does time on task over time really mean? And how much time are we talking about here? Hermann Ebbinghaus, in 1885, studied what would become known as the learning curve. Many researchers since have developed the time-on-task concept. Time on task over time has been among the most explored theories in the field of learning. In Malcolm Gladwell's book *Outliers: The Story of Success,* he presents the now-popular 10,000-hour-rule of achieving expert status in anything. 10,000 hours. Look it up. *Huffington Post* says it is a myth, that the 10,000 hour thing is half-true. Huff Post says it's the 50-hour, good-enough level "where amateurs and experts part ways." *Inman News* (add that to your must-read professional subscriptions) does the 10,000-hour math for us in "12 Tips for New Real Estate Agents": 3 hours a day, 5 days a week, that will roughly take you a decade.

My advice today is this. Start building up your knowledge base, start moving toward expertise status as quickly as possible, speed up your business metabolism, speed up your learning curve. We are not talking about perfection here. We are talking about getting better faster. Better is good. Perfection? She's annoying, fire her. (Unless she's a pharmacist or builds airplanes or is your bookkeeper—then definitely keep her on the team.) Commit to this, get started. Let's take a closer look.

In your first year, you should be dedicating a minimum of five hours per week to practice. Practicing scripts, dialogues, what to say, your buyer presentation, your seller presentation…practicing until you sound confident. And then practice more. Want to get there faster? Double your hours of practice. In medical school, it's see one, do one, teach one. Simply reading it once in this book or some other script source doesn't quite cut it. Watching one YouTube video, while hitting another area of your brain (the auditory cortex near your ears and the visual cortex in the occipital lobe in the back of the head), is just a start. Read it, say it, write it, practice it, use it. Your brain needs all of these angles to move the material from input to processing the input to storing it in a meaningful and accessible file folder in your memory, so you easily know what to say when you need it. Put in the time.

Here's an example of what the increased hours can do for you. I met a San Antonio agent at a workshop a few years back. Ed, he was really good. Genuine, confident, solid. The guy was so smooth with what to say and how to say it, his confidence filled the room. He appeared to be one of the more experienced agents in the room. We were doing an exercise where we practiced scripts in a rapid-fire manner. Our conversation went something like this:

Me: *"Ed, wow . . . you're really good. How long have you been in the business?"*

Ed: *"Two months."*

Me: *"No, how long have you been a licensed Realtor?"*

Ed: *"Two months."*

Me: [somewhat blank stare] *"Seriously? Two months? Were you an assistant or something before? I mean, you're really good. How did you do it?"*

Ed: *"They told me to do five hours a week of practice and role play. I'm really competitive, and I needed a paycheck faster than everyone else, so I've been doing fifteen."*

He was two months in, sounded like a pro, already had five or six clients lined up, and five or six additional leads in the pipeline. He was practicing what to say 15 hours every week. He got better faster than everyone else.

Note: the top agents in the country still practice years into the business. Put it in your calendar and stick to it. Be like Ed.

ACTION ITEM: YOUR CALENDAR IS MONEY!

Five hours per week. Let's keep this really simple. Get out your calendar. Pencil in five hours per week of practice. If you want the Ed approach, pencil in fifteen. For most people, this takes discipline and accountability. It's not like you have a boss who is checking in on your progress every day or every week. We will tap into this discipline and accountability topic throughout the book. For now, take five minutes and put practice in your calendar.

ACTION ITEM: CALL YOUR BIGGEST ADVOCATE, AGAIN

Yep, we already did this. And we're doing it again. That same person you called in Chapter 1, we're calling them again, and here's why. You need the close people in your life in your court.

Some of them will forget that you are in real estate. Some of them are holding back, waiting to see if you are really moving forward with this real estate thing.

Sometimes our closest people can be our biggest advocates *and* our biggest critics. So the conversation may be as simple as giving that important person an update on how you're doing. It may look something like this:

> "Hi. It's me. I wanted to give you a little report of how things are going at work. I want you to see how serious I am and tell you a couple things I have going on. Got a minute?

> "First, I really appreciate your support. So I [then go on to tell them about your open houses, the buyers you're working with, that as the national sales manager of your real

estate business you basically go to the office in the morning and do not leave until you have talked with x number of people about real estate . . . or some pertinent fact about what you're doing].

Then ask if you can practice a script or two with them over the phone.

"So I spend about an hour a day just practicing what to say, my presentations, and studying the market. I realized I would like a little real feedback, trying to get this to sound natural. I want to run this by you, get your feedback."

Then practice with them. They may laugh a little; they usually offer a little advice like "be yourself," then half the time they'll mention someone who may have a real estate need.

You always want to end with a question, something like this:

"Is there anyone you have come across recently who mentioned real estate?"

And then you need to train them HOW to help you:

"When you do hear of someone, don't just give them my card. Instead, say this: "You know what? I really want to introduce you to/have you talk to my friend [your name]. She's the friend I mentioned who is a Realtor. What's

*your e-mail? I'm just going to send an e-mail
that introduces the two of you. No pressure;
she'll treat you like family and may be able
to help you. At the very least, she'll be a
good resource."*

CHAPTER 12

BIRD DOGS AND YOUR NEXT FEW CLIENTS

FIVE PEOPLE

Over the years, I have observed a pattern in real estate where the majority of your leads and traction actually come from a few key people. These are your people who always seem to be digging up new potential clients for you and sending them your way, or drawing your attention to the opportunity. We'll call these your bird dogs.

So what is a bird dog? It is a hunting dog analogy for the people in your life who always seem to be spotting new client opportunities for you and your business. Bird dogs innately sniff out opportunities and point at them. Whether you hunt or not (I do not) or whether you own a Springer Spaniel, a German Shorthaired Pointer, or a Chesapeake Bay Retriever, even the couch-sitting kind, you need your bird dogs, your five opportunity-finding people.

I have helped many REALTORS® over the years evaluate their businesses. I still do today. Specifically, I help them evaluate the source of their business. Where are their leads coming from, and how can we make that work at a higher level? Time and time again, a pattern surfaces, a pattern of five people. Five key people and their introductions, their referrals, their referrals' referrals, their networks, and their support resulted in a significant chunk of the agent's clients.

I'll give you a personal example. Early on in my business I kept an insanely detailed spreadsheet of all my closed clients. This was both a money ledger and a demographic log. Columns included the basics of name, address, zip, price, commission, who the other Realtor was, the lender, where we closed it, and, most importantly, how that client found me. Annually and early on, I analyzed that data and realized that there were some key people who were sending me a lot of business. I recognized early on that I had a few bird dogs, and I shifted my perspective as far as taking care of them, feeding the relationship, and cultivating a few other relationships that had the potential of joining the VIP club.

Find Your Five People

Your five people and your next client opportunity, or the opportunity to increase your price point, may be closer than you think. Your key people could be your mother or your spouse, and his or her work network. Or your five may be in unsuspecting places—the guy you met at the coffee shop, the speech therapist at your kid's school, the quiet neighbor, your former boss.

My five people look like this:

1. My spouse. Knows everyone, retired teacher, has an antique business, super engaging on Facebook, always meeting and attracting people.
2. My financial advisor and her spouse. These two know a lot of people and are both in the business of helping people make sound financial decisions. They understand referral business at a core level. I support them, they support me.

3. My lender. My top lender has been a dear friend for 15 years or so. Big community leader, knows everyone. She always seems to be looking out for people I should know.

4. The Susan Arbuckle Band. Yep, friends with a popular local band that draw nice complementary crowds of more friends. They played at my business relaunch party, and together we sponsor a big annual community event. They always seem to be introducing me to the right people.

5. My Realtor network. This is a broad category on my list, but nearly 20% of my business comes from Realtor referrals around the country. My ability to love on these folks and stay top of mind is key to the sustainability of my pipeline.

I am always looking for the right opportunity to add to this list of five. But more importantly, I am always looking for the right opportunity to love on and double-down on these important people in my world. I would rather have my list of five and have that solid as a rock, than a list of 20 and have no one feel special.

Let's break yours down a bit:

5 PEOPLE: Who are five people you know who know everyone? (Write it down.)

5 PEOPLE: Who are five people who would give you the shirt off their back, who believe in you, who would not hesitate to help you if you asked? (Write it down.)

5 PEOPLE: Who are five people you know who started their own business or have done something professionally impressive? (Write it down.)

5 PEOPLE: What is your top community involvement or local network, and who are your favorite five people in that network? (Write it down.)

ACTION ITEM: FIND YOUR FIVE PEOPLE

You guessed it. The quick lists you just wrote down? Call them. Do yourself and your bank account a favor and do not move on to the next chapter until you have talked to these people, every single one of them. Call these people now.

Here's what to say:

"I promised myself I would call you today. Do you have a second?

Option 1: *"You know everyone. You probably know more people than anyone I know. That's why I'm calling. I have big goals for my business this year. Here's my quick and easy question: Who do you know that I should know?"*

Option 2: *"You love me, right? I need your help. I have big goals for my business this year. Here's my quick and easy question: Who do you know that I should know?"*

Option 3: *"You've started your own business/ you've accomplished some impressive things. That's why I'm calling. I have big goals for my business this year. Come have coffee with me. I want to ask you about your success, get advice for starting something new. I figure I should listen to successful people and you're on my short list. What is your availability this week or next?"*

Option 4: *"How can I help you? You have always been very supportive of me and my business. How can I help you? How is your business? What are you working on? Is there anyone I know that you would like to meet? Let's have coffee and catch up."*

BONUS MATERIAL

I want to get some extra material on the table. Not every single ACTION ITEM or exercise in this book will be your cup of tea. Find a couple of outlets that truly speak to you that actually sound like fun, and head in that direction. Here are a few options to consider.

ACTION ITEM: Local Businesses

Pop in to ten local businesses and introduce yourself. This can be especially helpful when it is an area of town that you regularly visit, or that you live in or near. Are you in a smaller town? Then stop by every single business. Focus on whatever it takes to get into conversations with people. And keep going back. Start building people's recognition of you as a Realtor, you as a hardworking Realtor. Sometimes it is as simple as a "Hello, it's your favorite Realtor again!" What if you started meeting all your favorite people and connections in the same coffee shop all the time, and you got to know the coffee shop owner and the staff?

Back to the pop-ins at the local businesses. Here's what to say:

"I live nearby, and I realized I did not know every small business in the neighborhood, so I thought I'd drop by and introduce myself. I am a Realtor who specializes in this area of town. Where do you live? Do you have a go-to Realtor? When you have a real estate question, who do you call? Do you have any real estate needs this year, or know someone who could use my services? Here's my card in case you hear of someone. Do you have a card? I appreciate your time. I'll stop by again. I like this place. What's the one thing I should know about your business? [listen] Great. I am going to send some business your way. Have a great day."

And note, you may want to buy something while you're there, if appropriate. That may work best for the coffee shop, gift store, or auto parts store, not so much for the car dealership. But speaking of car dealerships, when I bought my Mini Cooper in 2010, my sales guy, Charlie, turned into a client.

And then go back and go back and go back. And send a friend or two or three in there, and make sure they mention you with some form of "My good friend Susan, the Realtor, sent me."

Mentors

Remember, we're looking for and cultivating bird dogs, raving fans, champions, your five people, folks who simply have their radar up all the time looking for opportunities for you.

You've just started this new amazing chapter in your life...take some encouraging, experienced people along for the ride. Find a few mentors. Find a non-Realtor, someone who has accomplished some sort of business success that you admire. They could be retired, or full-on with big expansion. Ask them out for coffee or bring them lunch at their place of work.

Think of it this way. You are always building relationships and on the lookout for key relationships. Having some focus and intention around this will help, a lot, versus thinking it will just naturally happen. So identify some people in your world that you admire, and here's what to say:

"Alice, thank you so much for taking my call. I assume you're busy so I'll be brief. I just recently started my new business [or I am relaunching my business], and I promised myself that I would meet with one successful business pro or entrepreneur or interesting person every week for the next two months.

So that is eight amazing people, and you're on my short list. I intend to do this right. I just want to ask you how you got started, what advice you may have for someone just getting started, and if you were to do it all over again, what you might do differently. I figure in the process I'll end up with a couple of mentors (no pressure). I simply really value your opinion and experience and would be honored if you would meet me for a cup of coffee or, better yet, if I could bring sandwiches by your office sometime this week."

Friends

Friends who bought a home last year. I love this category for newer agents. It is a super low-pressure way to have a quality real estate conversation with a friend who already used another Realtor. Remember, we're looking for bird dogs, advocates, champions!

Call three (or one, or five, or ten) friends who bought or sold a home last year, and ask them a few questions about their experience. The call might go something like this:

"Hey, it's [me]. Got a minute? You guys have been in your new home . . . what, six months now? Awesome! How is it? You love it? What's your favorite thing about the house? Any projects you're working on? Hey, the reason for my call . . . you know I just started in real estate, right? (I love it . . . wish I had done this sooner.) My question for you has to do with your experience buying your house. Can I ask you a couple of questions? What did your Realtor do really well? What could he or she have done better? Is she still in touch with you? What was most important to you in the process?

*Do you have any questions on anything . . .
home warranty, property taxes, filing for your
homestead exemption? I can probably help,
and if I do not know the answer, I'll go get
it for you. No problem . . . call me anytime
you have any question on your home . . . need
a handyman, painter, plumber? I can help you.
Hey, real quick before I get off the phone,
is there anyone you know who may need my
services this year? I appreciate you keeping
me in mind. Hope to see you guys soon. Would
love to see the house."*

Why Should I Work With You?

Remember, this is a bonus section, and at this point we are going to cover a critical question: Why should I work with you? Why should I hire you? You better know the answer. Get clear on what you bring to the table. More importantly, get clear on how to confidently take control of this conversation.

This business is very much a skill-based business, and your ability to handle the most common objections will not only be a big confidence booster, it will help you convert your leads into actual clients.

Here is a starter list of some of the most common objections:

- Why should I hire you?
- I think we'll wait.
- Will you lower your commission?
- We're talking to two other Realtors.
- I have a friend who is a Realtor.
- We want to price it at $325k (when it's worth $290k).
- We want to offer $30k below the list price (when it's the

coolest home and the market and homes are selling for full price in three days).

- We're just looking.
- We're going to try to sell it by ourselves first.
- We're not ready to talk to a lender.

We address these objections in the script section at the back of the book. For now, here is my favorite response to the why-should-I-hire-you question:

"Why should you hire me? Maybe you should, maybe you shouldn't. I need to know more specifically what your needs are to make sure I am the right person and can deliver. You're interviewing me and I'm interviewing you; it needs to be the right match. What is your situation?"

Let's break down this response a bit.

- It's super honest.
- It is not salesy.
- It does not involve a monologue of my resume and skills.
- It's about them.
- It ends in a question that shifts the attention from me to them.
- It is offense, not defense...I took control of the conversation with the strategically placed what-is-your-situation question.
- You can address your skillset later in your buyer consultation, when you address some of the things you bring to the table to get the job done right.

CHAPTER 13

GOOGLY

Whether you are a social media hound who could qualify for the Snapchat Olympics, a hold-out who only recently upgraded to a smartphone, or a member of the social media love-hate category, your customers and potential customers are online, and they will check you out online before they pick up the phone and call you. Your friends will even do this to you. I cannot teach any class without spending a little time on this topic, and I certainly cannot complete this book without a review of how you need to show up online. It's a brief chapter, but let's cover a few important things.

Think of it as building your reputation online. You get to drive that bus.

Here's the deal. The first thing or the last thing prospective clients may do before they call you is check you out online. What if you don't look like a solid, serious real estate professional on a simple Google search? What if they cannot find your phone or e-mail with a simple Google search, or a click on your Facebook About Me link? I would hate to see you do all the pipeline-development work outlined in the previous chapters, then lose the client because your LinkedIn profile still says you are an account supervisor at ABC Company or a teacher at ABCDEF Middle School or working at Starbucks. You must look good and legit online.

FIND YOURSELF

While this could be a self-help mantra or an invitation to a spiritual retreat, in the context of your reading today, it is an invitation to find yourself online. Simple Google search. Try this: pretend you are someone, even a friend, who needs to quickly find your personal phone number and your e-mail address online. How many clicks does it take you to get that information?

Let's see how easy it is to find you online, how easy it is to find your basic contact information, if you actually look like a full-time real estate pro online. Regardless of your love or hate for social media, your disdain for mixing business and personal, your tight grasp on your other career or gig, or your need or desire for privacy, these are business tools and you need to be aware of how you are showing up online. If you choose to clamp down on your privacy online, just know that being a secret agent will cost you some business, and you'll need to make up for it in some other arena

Stop and actually do this simple online audit exercise. Tip: you may want to try this on someone else's computer, because your laptop and its cache and browsing history know who you are and where you've been.

- Google search:
    - Type in First Last Realtor (meaning your first name, your last name, and the word Realtor; hopefully I did not need to point that out) … how easily do you pop up on the top of the search results? And what does it say about you?
    - Type in First Last My Town, hit enter.
    - Type in First Last Brokerage, enter.
    - Type in your e-mail address, how many websites are you on?
    - Type in your cell phone, any results?

- Type in your old phone number or old email address, any results that need updating?

- Your Facebook About Me page—you need an e-mail, a phone number, and a website listed.

- LinkedIn—in today's online-driven world, you are expected to have a current LinkedIn profile. Do not fail this test.

- Your business website—is your information easily located? Is it only your broker's number and contact information, or are you easily found? I say this in particular because what if a friend of a friend is trying to find you online and, instead, lands on your broker's page and simply clicks the button to talk to an agent? Any agent. Or they click the form for more information, and that form either lands in the broker's inbox or goes to the agent on duty at the time? You may have just lost a lead without even knowing it.

Make sure you are aware of the rules and regulations in your area, state, and brokerage for how you identify yourself online. Compliance is a big deal. Your broker holds your license (and takes on liability on your behalf), and some state board issued that license (and their purpose is to regulate the industry and protect the public). So these important people and entities have a say, an important legal say, in what you do and how you present yourself, both in print and online.

Working through this exercise can help you find old information online. Clean it up, make sure you look good online, make sure you are compliant. One thing I did earlier in my career, and still do now and then, is search online for a top agent, or an agent I admire, or an agent that I know is pretty techy, to see how they are showing up. What websites are they on, how do they describe themselves in their bios? I do this to get new ideas for how to present myself, to find new websites that I should consider, and to simply study the top or coolest agents so I can have some awareness of how things are evolving online.

I am always sharpening and tweaking my presence online. It is never perfect, and I have little to no control over Google analytics or algorithms. But I do have control over my content. Oh, and you need a professional or professional-looking photo.

And don't fall for those solicitation e-mails or phone calls from some company that promises, for a bunch of money, to help you improve your ranking on Google. I swear I get one of those calls a week. Ugh. Don't do it.

ACTION ITEM: START YOUR BIO DOCUMENT

This to-do will save you a lot of time and frustration down the road. You are going to create a document that has two or three versions of your bio paragraph, as well as all of your critical url links. The beauty of having this document at your fingertips is that you never have to go on a hunting mission again to find your LinkedIn profile url, your Facebook business page url, or your NRDS ID number. And you maybe did not even know that you had an NRDS number, but some critical member profile page is asking you for it. (Hint, it's on your NAR member card and somewhere in your NAR profile.)

My bio file is a Word file, conveniently called "BIO.doc," and I have it pinned in my favorites list so it is super accessible. I reference this file all the time. It has three primary sections. First, ID numbers. Second, critical links. And third, every bio paragraph I have ever written. Here is a run-down of mine (yours will vary):

ID Numbers

- my license number
- my NRDS number
- my CRS member number

Links

- my main website url
- my blog url
- my personal Facebook url
- my business Facebook page url
- my LinkedIn public profile url
- my Twitter profile url
- my YouTube channel url
- the url for my main promotional video on YouTube
- my Google+ url
- my Pinterest url
- my Zillow profile url
- my Yelp business profile url
- my Inman News author page url
- my Instagram url
- my Skype handle

BIO

This section of your document will build and grow. I use this document any time I am filling out a bio on a new website or refreshing an existing online professional bio paragraph. This is so I don't have to rewrite it every single time and hope that it is as complete and brilliant as the last time I wrote one. Here is where you can start:

- Short - Write a 3-4 sentence version of who you are.
- Medium - Write a 2-3 paragraph version of who you are.
- Long - Write a longer version of who you are, including background, skills, areas of expertise, what you bring to the table, why you are in real estate, what's in it for the client, and wrap it up with some personal interests.

One tip is that you can go online, maybe in Zillow or your brokerage agent directory or LinkedIn, and look up other Realtors to find examples of well-written and interesting bios. No, you cannot copy and paste someone else's brilliant bio. You can, however, find inspiration, keywords, and examples of above-average well-written bios. What you will also find in this online treasure hunt are plenty of examples of poorly written or non-existent bios. You need to look good online.

And, for entertainment purposes, you will find plenty of really bad agent profile photos. Seriously, that fluffy boa feather thing went out in like 1985. And if your profile photo is sixty pounds lighter, 15 years younger, and three hairstyles ago, you may want to upgrade. It's called truth in advertising. Yes, I recommend a professional photo. But a cool, happy, personal photo will do on day one; you can upgrade later. I used an informal photo for years. The kiss of death online is no photo at all; don't be a bubble head.

CHAPTER 14

RINSE AND REPEAT

SEXY

Let's talk about all the cool reasons you got into real estate.

You get to help people, keep a flexible schedule, and be your own boss. You have no financial ceiling, you like negotiating, you love design and architecture, you get to look at cool houses, you have no rush hour. While your friends are in a cubicle, you're driving around town with the top down. You get to meet people in the middle of the day for coffee, you're looking at cool properties, studying design and architecture. You're helping people change their lives.

You may start the day off working in your pajamas. You may take every Thursday off. You get to meet the kids at school lunch every Friday and sponsor the monthly school field trip. Yesterday you took the kayak out at 3 PM because you felt like it. Your car is your office and you have this general sense of freedom on any given day. Life is good.

Let's call this sexy real estate. It's most likely what attracted you to real estate and is what the public thinks you do.

NOT SO SEXY

And then there is the not-so-sexy part of real estate. Anyone who has sat in on one of my classes has heard me give this speech, the sexy versus the not-so-sexy part of real estate.

It's called a job. It's the two to three hours per day, five days a week of lead generation and lead follow-up. A job.

This is the foundation of your business, the frontal cortex of real estate, the DNA of sales. Make peace with this.

The biggest mistake in real estate? Leading with sexy. You must lead with the job. Getting the most important things done first every day versus running a squirrel farm. What is my fastest route to a paycheck today? Do that first. Always do that first. This is being a good boss. Be a good boss.

RENEW YOUR JOY

He discovered his reset button early on & there were not many things that bothered him all the rest of his days just because of that.
— Storypeople

This is a particularly poignant topic for agents feeling a little stuck, pushing through a rough patch, questioning their career path, at a mid-year check-up, or simply hitting the reset button on their business. When I relaunched my business in 2017, this was where I started.

Answer these questions for yourself:

- Why did I get into real estate in the first place?
- What do I like best about real estate?

- What am I good at?
- Who is my favorite client ever?

Recommit to the joy.

Business, and life, works best when the joy factor is solidly in place. Life and relationships and business and clients, they have their ups and downs. If you have misplaced your joy, people (or your next potential client) can read that energy a mile away. And the opposite is true. When your joy factor is solidly in place, your next potential client can read that magic a mile away. If you ever find yourself out of sorts, off your path, with misplaced juju, questioning what you are doing, searching or re-searching for the meaning and the fun, take a deep breath and reconnect with why you started this in the first place.

Your joy, your energy, your eye contact, it all matters. It's your mindset, your personality capital, and it will have a tremendous impact on your traction and success. The right mindset will gain you clients, and the wrong mindset will cost you clients: this is sales 101. Find your joy.

BROKER SUPPORT AND BEING NEW

I believe broker support is key, so if you are not getting broker support or training, it could certainly impact your results. Before pointing any fingers, let's see how you're showing up.

Of everything that your broker is offering (whether in person or online), how much of that have you attended or plugged into in the last 30-60 days? Get clear on what your broker offers and how he or she can best help you. Success leaves clues, and the top agents train and train and train. Make sure you're plugging in.

Broker support takes many different forms. Primarily, there is training and coaching. Training is content and knowledge; coaching is business development. Training is skill; coaching is mindset and accountability. Training is understanding the many nuances of the real estate contract, negotiation, market, and process; coaching is obstacle maneuvering and building a lead pipeline.

Mentors, when available, tend to be transactional and limited in scope. Their job, for a fee, is to help you through your first handful of contracts, because you will have a hundred questions. The mentor's job is typically not to teach you the entire business and help you build yours; rather, it is to help you do a good job with your first few clients and contracts.

If you're not getting support and training and coaching and mentoring, then you may want to either shop brokers or find a nationally known training program (these can be expensive) and find the one that will support you at the highest level. Interview top tier agents on their advice for high achievement in real estate, and a lot of them will say get a coach. In the beginning of your career, you especially need solid support and training with your first five to ten clients and the hundreds of questions that you will (or should) have. And you need a model that helps you build your business.

TEAMS

Did you know that the model these days for the top-top-mega agents is a team format? The team format is a bit of a brokerage within a brokerage. The general structure is the lead rainmaker agent (usually the face of the team), an admin or two, and a buyer specialist or two. The biggest teams may have five to twenty agents on the team, and thousands of dollars pumped into online advertising and neighborhood marketing. The big teams crush it on the phones. The big teams are script masters. There may be some big teams in your market.

The reason I bring this up is that for some agents, starting on a team (versus starting as a solo agent) can make a lot of sense. Agents who desire more structure, agents who do not want to tackle every single aspect of the business, or agents who want to ramp up their skills and experience faster may want to consider joining a team.

With most teams, it may not be exactly what you expected with your shiny new real estate license. With teams, you will be on a very specific schedule, will be on the phones a lot, will be expected to learn specific scripts fast, and will be expected to convert leads into clients and produce. A new agent on a team is almost always a buyer specialist. It is possible that you may not have any seller opportunity on a team; the rainmaker is usually the listing specialist. Your broker may have team opportunities, and may have limitations on who qualifies for a team. Talk with your broker or interview with teams before you get started.

It is not a bad way to get started in real estate, and for some agents, it's the perfect place. For other agents, it's not anywhere close to what they want. If this interests you, do some research on the topic.

RINSE & REPEAT

Rinse and repeat. Rinse and repeat. Go back to Chapter 1 and just keep doing it and doing it and doing it. This is the not-so-sexy part of real estate. It's work. It's repetitive work. The sexy part starts when you have built a beautiful, healthy, and sustainable pipeline, and the referrals are consistently rolling in. Nail this foundational principle now—that you are in a lead generation business first and a real estate business second.

Your success in this business will have a heck of a lot to do with building your stamina around this simple principle, this core repetitive activity. Get on offense with this. You are always building your pipeline, you are always looking for and nurturing your next five leads.

Rinse and repeat, because there is so much material in this book that you could simply recycle all the ACTION ITEMS. And then recycle again. Do them over and over and over again, ten to fifteen hours per week, and that alone can build a successful real estate pipeline.

ACTION ITEM: YOUR FAV

Find your Favorite

Review all the ACTION ITEMS in each chapter (and there is an ACTION ITEM reference section near the end of the book). What did you like? Identify one ACTION ITEM that you really enjoyed. And then double down on this. Whatever you enjoyed the most will most likely produce the most opportunity. If all of your leads are coming from friends, then call friends today with this:

> *"Hey, it's [me]. Got a minute? I realized all my business so far has come from friends or their friends. It's the thing I like most about the business. In order to hit my goals this month, I need two appointments every week. Who do you know I should talk to?"*

If you have had FSBO luck so far, or you just like talking to for-sale-by-owners, try this:

> *"Hey, Mr. FSBO. It's John with ABC Realty. I specialize in helping FSBOs get their homes sold, so I wanted to check in and see how it's going, see if you have any questions. Can you tell me a bit about the home? Are you familiar with the two required disclosures for sellers? At what point do you think you'll consider hiring a Realtor for the job*

of selling your home? (I have a sign in my car right now. We could have the home on the market in no time.)"

You're enjoying open houses? Then book three a week. Remember with open houses that all it takes is one solid rapport-building conversation with one person. I just had this open house quality-versus-quantity conversation with a year-three agent the other day.

She had one particularly boring open house where one person came in. Well, it was the right person because they hit it off. But get this: when the agent called her back to follow up, crickets. No response. Three weeks later, she gets a call from a builder sales rep, saying the buyer just signed her up as their Realtor and they signed for a $400,000 new build. That same client then introduced her to her friend, which in turn led to an $870,000 purchase. That is over a million in production from one boring open house that had one visitor who initially did not return the phone call. Give the quality-versus-quantity open house a shot.

ACTION ITEM: IDENTIFY YOUR PROCRASTINATION

What did you miss? Identify one ACTION ITEM from the book that you either did not do (for whatever reason) or fell short on. Is there something you said you would do, but it remains untouched? Sometimes it's just a matter of building more skill in that particular area, then results start to show up. Run with one of the items you have been avoiding and get more conversations under your belt.

I am personally a fan of doing more of the things you enjoy versus forcing yourself to do the things you're avoiding. But in your first year or two, you need to push through the avoidance issues—or if you are in a relaunch, or in any particular stuck state of mind. After you identify the item or two that keeps taking up brain space as it remains undone, untouched, or avoided, you have a choice to make. Either remove it from your list or tackle it; either way, you'll remove it from your plate, which is the key result of this activity.

Pay attention to what you like, pay attention to what you are avoiding. Often, avoidance tends to correct itself with practice. If you're comfortable with what to say, you'll push through to new levels of competency.

For example, if you have been avoiding calling that one FSBO in your neighborhood, do this...march over there right now (put the book down) and knock on the door. Or do this: watch three YouTube videos on how to talk to an FSBO, spending more time on the video you like the most. Hit replay, replay, replay. Find the FSBO script section at the end of this book and write them out ten times, type them out yourself on your laptop (start a personal collection of your favorite scripts, edited to fit your style), record yourself on your phone saying the script, walk around the house for thirty minutes saying the scripts out loud, say them to the dog, say them with a funny accent, whisper them, say them in front of the mirror, practice them with your best friend or significant other. Help your brain absorb the information. In no time, you'll start sounding like, looking like, and feeling like an FSBO pro. Then get in the habit, starting immediately, of calling on and stopping by FSBOs. Start telling your friends and neighbors that you specialize in for-sale-by-owners, and ask them to text you the address and a photo of the sign when they see one.

> We are what we repeatedly do. Excellence then, is not an act, but a habit.
>
> — Commonly credited to Aristotle, but really the words of Will Durant, *The Story of Philosophy: The Lives and Opinions of the World's Greatest Philosophers*, 1926

ACTION ITEM: YOUR CALENDAR AND MY TRUE STORY

Let's revisit your calendar and those five hours of practice every week. Is it really on your calendar or did you blow through that chapter? An hour a day. Your confidence and your results will directly correlate to the amount of time you put into practicing what to say.

I am going to unpack this topic a bit. But first, I want you to take care of this simple action list immediately:

- Block one hour every day, Monday through Friday, and call it "practice." Put it in your calendar right now. That would be five hours per week. First thing in the morning is best. Treat this appointment as if it is one of the most important appointments on your calendar. It is an appointment with yourself. Tell yourself that you have to hit four of them; five is the goal for a perfect week, four minimum. Do this for a minimum of two months; more is better. Remember the rookie Ed who did 15 hours of practice a week? Do more hours for a couple of months if you intend to accomplish skill and confidence faster than the rest of the pack.

- For at least two of these daily practice appointments, set up a recurring appointment where you practice with another agent. This will be most time-effective if you do it over the phone. Try Skype or Facetime or Google Hangout. This agent becomes one of your accountability partners. If this practice partner starts becoming unreliable, missing more and more appointments, or gets off topic all the time, then fire them as your practice partner and find another with a commitment that matches yours. You may have to go through multiple practice partners until you find one as committed to mastery as you are. Your practice partner could be in another city or state. These practice appointments need to be on-task, and can be as little as twenty minutes if you are on-task. Limit the real estate chit chat and just practice what to say, role play with the other agent.

- Tell someone about this plan, this task, this goal. Someone in your household works nicely, or a good friend or family member or your broker. Tell them that you are telling them so that they'll help you stay accountable. When you tell someone else, you raise the bar on your seriousness and you increase the likelihood of hitting the goal.

- Print out a two-month calendar and post it on the wall somewhere. For every day that you hit your appointment, highlight the day. This way you have a visual of your progress, you become your own accountability partner, and anyone else living in your home or coming by your office will ask you about it.

True story, I did this to write this book.

6-8 AM, four to five days a week, for four months. I had gotten off track with my writing, immersed in my business, and had put the book aside for a while. If you are a writer or have a book in you, putting it aside for a while to simmer is actually a valuable tool, but at some point you have to have keyboard time. So I started with a July plan: my focus for the month, a theme for July. For the entire month of July 2017, I had this plan: alarm 5:50 AM, at my desk with coffee by 6 AM, perfect week five days, ten hours, minimum four days, posted on the wall, posted a video on Facebook talking about it, and kept at it until it was complete.

I did the calendar-on-the-wall exercise. I liked the task of highlighting each day I hit the 6 AM two-hour writing target. At one point, I shifted to 5:30 AM, and occasionally 5, as I needed to log more keyboard time.

Occasionally, I got off track, but I had three accountability partners who would ask me how I was doing with my writing program. And, get this...because of the Facebook video I posted? I really had about 400 accountability partners. I posted that video on Facebook for a couple of reasons. One, I knew it would help motivate a few people to tackle a project, and two, it would raise the bar on my own accountability. It accomplished both.

I am not super hard-wired for this sort of push. I had to be very intentional about it. Sure, I have a history of getting things done, and I have all sorts of athletic training in my past. So it may look, on the surface, like this comes naturally. That would be an illusion.

I am not the most disciplined person on the planet. I love a shiny object or twelve. I need some structure. In team sports, the team is the structure. But in solo situations, like the long-distance runner or the writer or the person learning to play the guitar, most of us need a tool or two in place to help us put in the hours, to help us produce and accomplish. I needed to build in a tool to help me produce. So what do you need?

Some of you reading this book are crazy hard-wired for discipline and structure, you have savant-level get-things-done built into your DNA. This will be an easy section for you. And, frankly, you may have clients faster than everyone else because of your discipline, your record of getting the most important things done first every day. You're built for sales.

Most of you reading this book are a bit like me. You're capable of discipline, but given a choice, you're off doing all sorts of other things. You are shiny-object oriented, so some structure is supercritical. If you are like me, a little structure and accountability can go a long way.

Some of my friends commented on my Facebook video, the video about this 6 AM writing project, with things like "your discipline is inspiring!" The reality is, my discipline is a challenge.

Until it becomes a habit.

The best-selling book, *The ONE Thing: The Surprisingly Simple Truth Behind Extraordinary Results*, by Gary Keller and Jay Papasan, nails this topic. This book is a must-read for any new endeavor, a must-read for changing the trajectory of your life, a must-read for shifting from shiny-object mode to getting things done. Ever wonder why some people get so much more done than others? It's a bit of an illusion. Read the book.

CHAPTER 15

WHERE ARE THEY NOW - REMEMBER THE AGENTS IN CHAPTER 4?

Remember the stories at the beginning of the book? The vignettes of REALTORS® just getting a start? Let's fast-forward and see where they are today.

STEPHANIE: Newly Divorced Mama Bear

Stephanie is in her fifth year, has earned two industry certifications, and just sent one of her daughters off to college. She hired some administrative help (contract-to-close, marketing) and is consistently earning six figures. The majority of her business comes from her inner circle, a tight network of lifelong friends.

WILLIAM: Building A Life

William is looking for land west of town to build a home and get his boys into a top rated school district (and baseball program). His real estate success is creating that financial opportunity. For William, everything is about doing the right thing, keeping his mama happy, and providing a solid foundation and future for his boys.

William continues to network with the old men, the founders, in east Austin. He recently spoke at the Elks Club regarding east Austin real estate trends. One of the east Austin founders, one of the old men, believes so much in what William is doing that he wants to set up a college fund for William's boys. As I reread this, it sounds a bit fairy tale, but it's true. William is an inspiration. As I write this, William is still just in his second year in real estate, just closed on his second flip, and is on track for six million in sales. He sees himself having an administrative assistant and a buyers' agent, a team, within a couple of years, and adding west Austin new construction to his repertoire.

MELANIE: VP Level Marketing Pro

Melanie is in her sixth year in the business and has steadily increased her sales, and her price point, year after year. Slowly and steadily. A brainiac and analyst, Melanie runs circles around market statistics and can recite current economic trends with ease. She is definitely a market expert. She sold her west Austin home and purchased a contemporary new build in trendy central Austin. While Melanie covers most of the greater Austin metropolitan area, I can see that her geographic focus continues to narrow a bit into the neighborhood she now calls home. That narrowing of focus is not only common, it makes business sense, is efficient, and allows Melanie the pleasure of building a geographic niche. Melanie has another niche with mid-century modern and contemporary design homes.

SAM: 60-something Non-profit Executive

I wanted to make sure I included at least one story of a new agent who, after a few years in the business, chose not to renew his license. This is not uncommon, even for a successful newer agent. Choosing not to renew, to leave the business, is not failure. Sam was succeeding in real estate, he was building a decent pipeline. He had skills, was a good advocate, a solid negotiator, was plugged in. Problem was, he wasn't loving the business. He didn't like it as much as he thought he would. I had coffee with Sam recently to better understand his story.

I asked him what happened...why the shift back into the job market? He immediately told me about a couple of buyer clients who ran him ragged, were tough as nails, sucked the oxygen out of rooms. The buyers were frustrated, and joy was seriously elusive in the process of finding the right home, negotiating, and navigating the process. Every Realtor knows this scenario. Sam quickly said that it wasn't that he couldn't handle a tough client, he understood that was part of the package. Rather, the joy-deprived experience with these particular back-to-back buyers helped Sam realize that his motivation for succeeding in real estate was not big enough to push through some of the more challenging aspects of the business. He truly wanted to make a difference in people's lives, and while real estate provided the opportunity to do so, it did not match Sam's version.

A few other things Sam said are worthy of note. He said he should have done more due diligence before he started in real estate. "I didn't know teams existed. If I had known teams existed, I would have seriously considered that path. I do not lean entrepreneurial, I work better in a team environment."

Another thing he noted was that his three years in real estate had too much emphasis on cold calling. "It wasn't the right model for me." The ironic thing here is that teams tend to follow the high volume phone model. Sam felt a more relational model would have been a better fit for him: higher quality conversations, more personal connections. While Sam was succeeding in having a high volume of conversations every day, he said he failed with follow-up. He said he was good at initiating the conversation, and pretty much sucked with follow-up (his words). My immediate thought on this dynamic was that if the conversations had been with people he actually knew, had some relationship with, some rapport, a referral from a friend, or someone he had clicked with at an open house, that Sam's follow-up would have come easily and naturally. Follow-up with cold calls, it's a numbers game. Follow-up with referrals, friends of friends, former colleagues, it's common courtesy. In the midst of his third year, the numbers game was wearing thin for Sam.

Sam is sincerely grateful for his three years in real estate—the training, the opportunity, and how he developed as a professional. And he is happily back in the nonprofit world.

The Roadmap

Throughout this book, I have attempted to share a variety of new and launching and relaunching agent stories, so you can find the one or two that resonate with you: your experience, your personality, your goals, your place in the world. In my two decades in this business, I have found that the larger body of real estate training material and advice and speakers and podcasts was so heavily laden with top 1% stories, with savant-level success stories, with mega this and super successful that, that agents who struggled their first year or two (which is almost everyone) or agents who had moderate financial goals were often questioning if they were good enough, or thinking that they had to become someone or something they were not to be successful in this business. It's like looking at a fashion magazine and only seeing supermodels. Where are the models with gray hair or the models who fit into a size twelve? Can you at least show us photos of the supermodels when they were in high school, before they were super?

Don't get me wrong. Those top 1% superstar stories represent some of the best practices in this business, they provide an inspiring vision of what is possible, and they are worthy of your time. When studying an industry, look at the best practices, not the average practices. But where are you at right now in your business, and what advice, motivation, tools, and action do you need to move forward?

> *Acting like something you're not is not only emotionally, spiritually, and frequently financially exhausting, it's unsustainable.*
> — Danielle LaPorte, *The Fire Starter Sessions*

I believe you have to see yourself in the mix, in the shoes, in the story. While the top 1% may motivate and inspire you, where is the roadmap for years one, two, and three, the roadmap to starting over? There are times when you have to stretch yourself beyond your current framework. Is there a mismatch between your current state of being and your goals? There are more times when you have to get in touch with your authentic self, capitalizing on what you do best, what you like, what you're good at, your style, your DNA. Be you. The old adage of "be true to yourself" applies here. Merge that mantra with "Who do I have to become to meet my goals?" and you create a pretty powerful balancing act and success formula.

Let's sum this up. Here are some of the key points, the roadmap, for starting or re-starting:

- Find clients fast.
- Take action that matters.
- Practice doing vs. studying.
- Have conversations every day.
- Track it.
- Call your mother.
- Follow your joy…do more of what you like to do, do more of what comes naturally, double down on what is already working.
- Check your power score. How are you showing up?
- Don't be a lousy boss.
- Review your top 100, your most likely source of clients and referrals.
- Know what to say: practice.
- Stay in touch with your bird dogs.
- Attend to the J.O.B. first.
- Remove shiny objects.
- Build in accountability.
- Be you.

If you stick to these basics with a sense of urgency, I would bet on your success. Let's reflect back on this foundational premise: you are in the process of creating something amazing in your life, your success will change the world. My sacred mission is to help you do that.

ACTION ITEM: WRITE IT DOWN

This ACTION ITEM is introspective and practical. Research shows that writing down your goals, as opposed to just keeping them in your head, significantly increases the likelihood of you actually hitting that goal. Empirical evidence and all: Dr. Gail Matthews, a psychology professor at the Dominican University, found that the likelihood of hitting your goals increases a whopping 42% if you write them down. So let's do that.

If you have not yet done so, put some words down in your journal addressing the following:

- What success looks like to me:
- What success will do for me and my family:
- My financial goals are:
- My personal goals are:
- My five-year vacation plan is:
- Here's how I will change the world:
- My sacred mission is:

CHAPTER 16

GET YOUR LICENSE! CHOOSE YOUR BROKER! REASSESS YOUR BROKER!

If you are pre-license or are considering changing brokers, this section is for you, and is super practical. This chapter will read a bit different than the others in that it is very specific and detailed and technical. There is a ton of detail to consider when you are getting your license and choosing a broker, and I am attempting to provide that detail and a bit of a roadmap in this chapter. If you are already licensed and considering changing brokers, then you can skip directly to the "Choosing a Broker" heading in a few pages.

Moving toward getting your license, let's take a closer look. First, a little English lesson.

REAL-TOR

There are two syllables in the word REALTOR®, not three. Whether you are in Michigan, NYC, or the Deep South, drawing it out to three syllables, ree-luh-tor, is inaccurate.

Speaking of vocabulary, let's cover some industry lingo. Realtor, salesperson, agent, broker, broker associate, associate broker, managing broker, manager, team leader...professional titles vary from state to state, and some of the lingo can vary from firm to franchise. Remember that the term Realtor is trademarked and reserved only for those persons who are members of the National Association of Realtors (NAR). You can get your real estate license and not join NAR, but then in most cases you would not be eligible to join your local board and participate in the multiple listing service (MLS). If you are looking at traditional real estate, NAR membership is part of the package.

IT TAKES HOW MUCH TIME?

The fastest I have seen someone get their real estate license is about two months. In this fast scenario, it is pretty much forty hours a week of classes and studying and hustle to move through the process. Most folks take longer, and this will vary considerably from state to state. Just yesterday, I ran into a Realtor friend who has recently moved from Texas back to California. She said she filed her CA license application six weeks ago and is still waiting. In some states, it is way too easy to get a real estate license (many industry pros think we should raise the bar of entry). Other states can involve a lot of time, steps, classes, background checks, fingerprints, forms, fees, bureaucratic runaround…all in the name of protecting the public from bad or unprepared or unethical real estate people, which is always a good idea.

The overall licensure timeline, which can vary from state to state, will typically include:

- License Classes - This may take a month, or it could take a year, depending on your focus. If you are still assessing if you want to move forward with licensure and real estate in general (you have read this far in the book, which is an indication that you are moving forward), consider taking one or two of the required classes, dipping your toe in the pool to see if you like it. Most agents take the majority of their classes online and then often an in-person exam preparation class right before they are ready to take the state and national exam. Depending on if they accept any of your college credits, you may have anywhere from 4 or 5 to maybe 8 to 10 classes to take. These classes will include topics such as principles 101, contracts, law, finance, ethics, and the national exam prep. Keep in mind that most real estate license classes only help you pass a test (that is what they are supposed to do), and most of them do not teach you how to survive and thrive in the business. Pass a test prep, yes. Understand nuance, market analysis, and business 201 of how to be a real estate rock star, no.

- License Test - Any real estate school where you are taking your license classes (whether online or in person), will help you understand your state license procedures and how to move through that as expeditiously as possible.

- License Application - In most states, you can begin this process before you have taken all of your classes. This is typically a good idea, as most state licensing boards will need time to do a background check, maybe fingerprints, and in most cases assess college transcripts to see if your college credits can take the place of any of the licensure credit requirements. This will vary considerably from state to state.

- License Acceptance - I have no idea how efficient your state is, but until they push the button that says that you are now licensed, then you cannot function as a real estate pro. This may or may not happen somewhat simultaneously with this next item.

- Broker Choice - You may have known from day one what broker was going to hold your license. You may still be assessing your options. But typically, the state will hold your license in some sort of inactive status until you tell them what broker to send your license to. This involves two pieces: one, the broker/brokerage, and two, the state licensing entity. Your broker will guide you in this process; they may have a specific form or required signature to make things happen at the state level.

- Local Board Application - This is the typical flow of things, that once you are properly set up with both the state and your broker, then you are joining the local board, including your multiple listing service (MLS) subscription. In most cases, this happens somewhat simultaneously (and hopefully online).

Talk with your local resources, the local board, your real estate school, brokers, and the state to get clear on the smoothest process in your area. And of course, most of these steps involve money.

MONEY - IT COSTS HOW MUCH?

Every Realtor has gone through the fee-at-every-step experience of getting licensed. In most cases, you will pay for all of these, not your broker. In this section, I am going to outline some generalized costs so you can be realistic and prepared before you spend a dime. I have seen a handful of agents over the years have an actual "investor" help them get started in the business. In most of these cases, the "investor" was grandma or mom and dad helping a young professional get started. New businesses get started with seed money all the time, so why would your new career be any different? If someone is going to help you financially, be prepared to present them with a bit of a business plan of how much you need, what it goes toward, your plan to gain your first twenty clients, and your plan to pay the investor back. Most folks will fund this effort on their own.

First, a little perspective on the cost of getting started in real estate. There is pre-license, license, memberships, and dues, and then the ongoing expense of actually running and marketing your business. Compared to almost any other business out there on the planet, it is relatively inexpensive to get started in real estate. Besides your car, your smartphone, your laptop, your license, your time, and an appropriate wardrobe (except in maybe Key West), there are pretty much no asset requirements to getting started in this business. If you were to start even a taco stand, a lawn service, or a children's clothing line, you would invest some serious funds into equipment, inventory, and space. So if you have any sort of gag response to the expenses outlined below, you may need to reassess or save up.

Let's take a closer look at fees and then we'll add it up at the end. These are generalizations designed to give you a budget framework. I would always pad it a little to leave room for unsuspecting or supplemental fees that either no one told you about or you missed on the website or in the fine print.

Licensure Classes $400 - $1,500

Again, things vary greatly from state to state. You may be required to take three classes, or ten, or somewhere in between. With a simple perusing of online real estate schools and clicking on various states, I can see 180 classroom hours required in Texas, 135 in California, 90 in Minnesota and Oklahoma, 75 in Illinois, 60 in Iowa and Virginia. Each of those states then have varying numbers for continuing education hours required in your first and second years, required for your first license renewal. Those numbers can change at any time, so do your homework and do not rely on this paragraph as the license hour bible.

In most locations, you will have options of in-person classes and online classes. You get to choose the option that works best for you. The online classes tend to be cheaper. Ask other agents in your area what they recommend for taking the license classes. Some of these real estate schools will offer some sort of discount if you also sign up (and pay for) the package deal that includes your first year continuing education classes.

License Application $200 - $400

Let's use Texas as an example. In September 2017, I found these fees on the Texas Real Estate Commission license fee page:

Sales Agent Application	$205
Fingerprint Fee	$37
Background Check Fee	$27
Real Estate Recovery Fee	$10
Paper Processing Fee	$20

This is just one example. Your state may be cheaper, may be more expensive. I do find, true to form with most government websites, that it can be easier to understand all the fees by referencing either the real estate school material or the brokers' informational recruiting packets versus the state agency website. The schools simply tend to spell it out in an easily understood format, versus putting together a Rubik's cube flowchart of if/then fee structures that take a half dozen clicks to find.

Board & MLS $1,000 - $1,600

Austin Board of Realtors, Metropolitan Indianapolis Board of Realtors, Des Moines Area Association of Realtors, Marathon And Lower Keys Association Of Realtors, these are all examples of the local boards you will join in order to practice in your area and join the multiple listing service (MLS). Some agents will join more than one board, especially if they live on a state border. Most of my New York City Realtor colleagues also have some sort of membership in New Jersey.

Again, do not rely on these numbers as the fee bible. I am providing these after considerable clicking around and as examples of what to expect. Fees are subject to change and

I may have missed a fee or two. Some Board web sites are certainly much easier to navigate and more informative than others.

Here is an example from the Austin Board of Realtors:

Primary Membership Application fee	$200 (one-time fee)
Orientation fee	$25 (one-time fee)
ABoR Dues	$125 (annual)
NAR Dues	$120 (annual)
Image campaign	$35
TAR Dues	$117 (annual)
Legal	$5
Mobilization	$5
Total	$632
MLS	$309 (semi-annual)
eKey	$117 (semi-annual)

And, after much clicking, an example from the Omaha Area Board of Realtors:

New Realtor Application Fee	$150
Local	$165
State	$230
National	$155
Total	$550
MLS	$30 (per month)

Broker $0 - $500

Does the broker have any one-time new agent set-up fees? Any new agent training fees? Or a fee for the training manual? Are their classes free? What are their monthly expenses? Do you pay for an office? Is there a technology fee? Is there a per transaction fee? Do you pay an errors and omissions fee (E&O) with every closing (most do)? And, of course, what is the commission split? Or is it a fixed amount per month? Or a per transaction fee? Or some combination thereof? For as many brokerages as there are out there, there are varying commission and fee structures.

And what do you get for your money? I believe you get what you pay for. Keep in mind that your broker has to run a profitable business, and that the broker takes on liability on your behalf. Any time someone takes on liability on your behalf, it's expensive.

Some concrete things that have been important to me over the years in terms of what I was paying for with my broker are that I wanted quality education, an open environment with freely shared information, an effective and trendy website, and current technology. Your needs may be different. Your needs may change over time. Some agents simply want the absolute bare bones, lowest cost option. No judgement here; figure out what you need, assess your options, and then be open to the possibility that your needs may change tomorrow or over time.

Totals $1,500 - $4,000

Is it more than you thought or about right? You are starting a new business, so plan ahead. What exactly are the costs in your area? Then pad it some—heck, double it, because I promise you there will be costs that you did not anticipate or that come at you like mosquitos at a Fourth of July picnic.

Commission Structure, Do The Math

As for how we get paid, there are different models and variations out there. There are fixed fee, per transaction, split, split on a scale, capping, salary (as in you are actually an employee versus an independent contractor), teams, and whatever you can negotiate with your broker options. There are brokerages with heavy expenses, staff, services, brick and mortar, there are lower expense cloud-based firms, and there are zero service low fee firms that tend to be a place where agents who are not doing any business park their license.

Whatever commission structure options you are staring down, do the math. Do YOUR math. On the surface, the commission structure being offered may seem attractive when comparing brokers around town, but how does it play out with different sales scenarios? You will benefit from running sample projections of split, cap, and fixed costs on a spreadsheet of how the different options play out. What is your take if you sold $1 million in sales, $3 million, $5 million, $8, $10, $12, $20 million? For example, a 90/10 split in perpetuity may be attractive for the $1-$3 million sales volume range, but a 70/30 split that "caps" at $2 million (you get 100% after $2 million for the rest of that year) will pay out way more to the agent at a higher sales volume. Or if the broker commission split never caps, that can be very expensive to the higher-producing agents.

Let's look at "cap" a little closer. The cap means that once you sell a certain amount of real estate in one year, then you get to keep 100% of the commission the rest of the year, usually with some per transaction fees. Cap can be expressed in either sales volume, such as a "two million cap"—you cap after you close $2 million in sales (four $500,000 homes)— or can be expressed in what you pay to the broker, such as a "$16,000 cap," meaning, as soon as you pay the broker $16,000, then you're done paying the broker for the remainder of that year. In one brokerage the cap will vary from city to city, depending on how expensive it is to run an office in that city (for example, it is more expensive for a national franchise to run an office in San Francisco than it is for the same franchise to run an office in Des Moines). I have seen caps as high as $40-60k. Some brokerages, such as eXp Realty, have the same cap no matter where you live.

Remember, you get what you pay for (or at least you should). Your low cost options may not have the tools and training and technology that you need to look good and gain momentum. If commission structure is your main brokerage choice determinant, then you may be starting your career with financial blinders. Personally, I would assess every other broker attribute first, and commission last.

Remember this basic financial premise...a brokerage is running a business, takes on liability on your behalf, and has to be profitable. The lowest split cheapest brokerage option out there in your town may not offer anything in return and may not have a sustainable business model. You get what you pay for.

60-90 Day Pay Cycle

The best case scenario in traditional real estate sales is that you may have a paycheck sixty days after starting. That would happen *if* you wrote and executed a contract within two to three weeks of starting with your brokerage and *if* that contract saw its way all the way to the closing table and key exchange. Just because that client is under contract to purchase or sell, doesn't mean the buyer's financing approval holds or that the home meets the lender's appraisal requirements or that the buyer's other home in Ft. Lauderdale closes on time. What if the Ft. Lauderdale buyer loses his job or buys a new car at the last minute?

Every seasoned Realtor on the planet has learned that you cannot bank on any single closing. You have to line them up for financial stability. If you are financing your life moving from commission check to commission check, let's just agree that it's stressful. If one deal falls through and you were relying on that to pay your rent or mortgage or credit card or to take the family on vacation, if this becomes any sort of pattern, it can chase you right out of the business or back to Grandma for an extension on her investment in your future.

Six-month Reserve

I have seen brand new agents start with very little and have seen brand new agents start with a $10,000 first-year marketing budget. I have seen brand new agents have to scratch and claw and continue working night shifts at the bar downtown to get their bills paid (some make it, some don't; truth: some of the top agents in the country started this way) and other brand new agents with little to no financial concerns.

You can easily find variations on the right number for your reserve or cushion in getting started. Four to six months will be the most common advice.

Here are the basics...add up your monthly basic living expenses, and make sure you have a solid cushion that could cover your expenses for four to six months. And then work your tail off to not touch that reserve.

VITAL RESOURCES

A quick online search for the licensure process in your state will be the best place to start. I would look for both the state licensing entity (Texas Real Estate Commission, California Bureau of Real Estate, Iowa Professional Licensing Bureau), and well-known real estate schools. The school websites tend to be a little easier to navigate and understand versus the official state websites, but you should definitely set your eyeballs on both.

A quick note on schools and going with a private real estate school vs. actually getting college credit in the real estate program at the local community college. The private school will usually be cheaper and a great deal faster. These private schools can typically get you through all of the required classes for your state in under six months. Community college programs, while perhaps more in-depth and possibly a greater learning environment, can easily take a year or two, depending on how often they offer each class and if they have sequential requirements.

Here are some simple resources that can help you get started:

- **realtor.com** is the website for the National Association of Realtors® (NAR). Someone who has a real estate license without joining NAR is an agent vs. a licensed (and trademarked) Realtor. This site has a blog loaded with articles to guide you.
- **Google** "how to get a real estate license in my state." I know, this is so basic I almost did not type it out. Fill in the blanks for the following:

  - My state licensing entity:
  - My local board and MLS source:
  - My local real estate schools (brick and mortar):
  - My top online real estate schools:

CHOOSING A BROKER, CHANGING BROKERS

This alone is a huge topic and you will benefit from some introspection, needs analysis, and homework. My coach calls it finding your belonging place. Your professional belonging place can change from time to time, as your vision for what you need and want can shift over time. It can be seriously affirming to go through a period of reassessing your brokerage choice, and realizing you're in a good place that supports you and your business principles and vision. I swear I reevaluated my broker choice every year or two in the business. Perhaps a bit like renewing your vows—sometimes a light exercise, sometimes more in depth, but it was always reaffirming to come out of that inner dialogue with a recommitment to my professional place in the world. In 2017, my reevaluation was major (I was itchy and my needs had changed) and led to a big move, a brokerage change. I'll get into that in more detail here in a bit.

Let's tackle the topic for the newly licensed first, then I'll run through some guidance if you find yourself in the I-am-considering-changing-brokers category. First, a little disclosure...I have my biases. Typically, we all have biases based on our experiences. I have purposefully laid out the majority of this book with little mention of specific brokerages (a little here and there for clarification). This section is different and I will tap into some specifics on a couple brokerages I know well. Bottom line is I want you to do YOUR research and find YOUR place.

Keep this business fundamental in mind...brokers are running businesses, and besides profit and investors and owners and stock valuation and quality customer service and reputation, there are two main factors that are foundational to real estate brokerage success. One is listing market share (homes for sale by that brokerage), the other is agent count. Besides serving and attracting the consumer (buyers and sellers), listings and agent count drive the broker side of the business. And agent count drives listings count. So agent count is the biggie. And then per agent production. Because of that, there is a lot of "recruiting" in the industry.

I have a little issue with recruiting. When recruiting is a big numbers game (think of a corporation that has to meet its sales quota), agents and brokerages do not always make the right decision. Whether new in the business or considering moving brokerages, remember you need to find your belonging place. Are you being recruited, or is the brokerage conversation consultative in nature? It should be consultative and information-based. You need to find the right place for you to build your business and lay the financial foundation for you and your family.

Here is part of my bias disclosure…I ran the largest single office new agent training program for the largest brokerage in the country for five years at Keller Williams Realty in Austin, Texas. At any given time, there were 100+ first-year agents in my program. I have lived the majority of my professional life in a large franchise environment that is all about training and coaching. So it is ingrained in me that training is important. And it is very important in this enormous and ever-changing business.

A lot of the big firms do training well; KW, Coldwell Banker, eXp Realty, and others have the training credential down in a big way. There is a three-generation California firm, Tarbell Realtors, that has had a big reputation for training in southern Cal. Keller Williams Realty has won *Training Magazine's* top training organization award more than once. eXp Realty's training is extensive and in the cloud, available 24/7. Many firms have excellent training and mentoring programs, some have very little. Do your research and identify the opportunities in your area.

And here is the second part of my bias disclosure…in 2017, I moved my license to eXp Realty. eXp was founded in 2008 and I had been watching this innovative brokerage. The eXp model shifts away from the traditional real estate model. eXp is agent-owned, cloud-based, publicly traded (I like stock options), and has made training and coaching extremely accessible in their online campus. Part of the draw for me was the culture and the people; that was first. Then the next big draw was the technology. Because their expenses are so much lower than brick-and-mortar brokerages, they are able to sock some serious resources into their technology and delivering on that model. This also allows them to provide stock options (agents are owners) and a revenue share program (passive income). I did a crazy amount of research when I was considering making the move. I look forward to a sustainable future in my new belonging place.

Literally, you could talk with every broker in your area. And maybe you should. Who are the players in your area? Who is up and coming? Who do you know? Who is hiring? Are there stock options or opportunities for passive income? What is important to you? I personally would talk to numerous brokers of all sizes and shapes and the agents who work with them.

In talking with other agents, be selective and be prepared to screen their feedback. I have found that if the dominant tone in the thread is negative and complaint-filled, then I am talking to the wrong person and I want out of that conversation. Right topic, wrong person. Seek out objective professionals, who will help you see the values, versus the disgruntled who thrive on throwing the competition under the bus. Gather your information, then talk with the brokers or their managers directly. I can personally introduce you to either Keller Williams or eXp Realty, and when I sponsor you to one of these firms, then I am invested in your success.

Talk with agents and brokers, gather your information, then decide for yourself. You are looking for YOUR belonging place and the right place with the right tools to build YOUR business.

Analyze your needs, do your research, find your place.

Choosing a Broker, Newbies

Of course you want to make a sound decision with your brokerage affiliation as you are establishing the foundation for your business, your branding, your marketing, your initial training and mentoring, and even your reputation. For brand new agents, let's cover a couple of important brokerage differences.

First, for a number of reasons, not all brokerages accept brand new agents. So the coolest, sexiest, most high-end brokerage in town may not be hiring. Some firms may or may not take new agents because they do not have the appropriate first-year high-touch program in place. Or you may be required to be in the mentor program for a year, or six transactions at a higher split. The small local broker may not be hiring unless you are a relative or your sister is the Mayor. They may not be set up to train and mentor new agents, or the broker may not want to take on the liability and the time commitment of the newly licensed.

I personally think your first brokerage (not that you would necessarily have a second broker, especially if your initial choice was a grand slam) should have a training, education, mentoring, and/or coaching program solidly in place. I have seen many new agents get started with little support (they chose the wrong broker or did not plug in) and they were still searching for a foundation one and two years in. Your license classes simply helped you pass a test, now you need to learn the business.

Remember this important concept; it would be rare for your real estate license classes to have effectively covered local real estate, lead generation, database, marketing, market analysis, market and economic dynamics, new construction ins and outs, contract nuance, commercial versus ranch versus condo versus land, estates, divorce, joint tenancy, the title process, property taxes, and leasing background checks. Your license classes did not cover what to say, how to handle the most common objections, repair negotiations, wood rot, flashing, plumbing static tests, pet odors, broken window seals, old roofs, how to be an open house pro, how to talk to an FSBO, how to market luxury properties, or how to handle distressed properties and distressed owners. What do you do if there is an unresolved insurance claim on the property? What if the buyer's funds are in a foreign country? What if the real estate agents miss one critical deadline in the contract? Your license classes certainly, or very rarely, covered the bigger stuff of how to be an entrepreneur, how to set up your finances and taxes, technology musts, how to manage the challenging work/life balance in real estate, and on and on and on. Really, I could go on and on.

As a new agent, you need help. Do a little research and find out who in your area has a solid training, mentoring, coaching program. Ask questions about exactly what is involved and how much it costs.

Are you assigned a mentor who doesn't really have time? Are you attached to a senior agent for a 50/50 commission split for your first five transactions? Are you more or less on your own? How often do they run their classes? Who teaches the classes? Are the classes and resources in-person or online? Who do you turn to for all of your questions? How available is that person? Will your broker be there to help you, or are they super busy and occupied with buyers and sellers? There are managing brokers who work directly with buyers and sellers (or often just sellers), and there are managing brokers who only manage the office.

Changing Brokers, Maybe

If you are in the considering-changing-brokers category, be careful with the grass-looks-pretty-green-over-there concept and do your homework. I have seen agents shift to another brokerage, only to return two or six or twelve months later with some form of "it wasn't what I thought." It is certainly possible that the best brokerage for you is your current broker. Or is it? Take some time with this.

It can be costly to hop from broker to broker. The cost for broker-hopping is not so much the hard costs you may encounter, such as a fee your state or board may charge to file with a new broker, or a new agent admin fee the brokerage may charge. Rather, changing brokers may have higher costs as in the cost of your time, and changes to your marketing. The biggie could be whether you get to take your listings with you or not. In most states, it is the broker who "owns" the listings. Those listings you worked so hard to obtain. Technically, the seller signed an agreement with the broker. If you change brokers, what is the broker's policy on releasing listings? Many brokers will not release the listing. They will assign it to another agent, maybe agree to pay you a portion, and then wish you well on your professional journey. So if you have multiple listings, you need to somewhat discreetly understand how this could impact you financially and plan accordingly.

Changing brokers can work in your favor with your friends, sphere, and database. When I switched to eXp Realty in 2017, it was a good excuse to reach out to my people with a powerful "I have a big announcement" marketing push. Facebook and LinkedIn played nicely in getting the word out with my announcement. It energized my business and stirred up curiosity, interest, and leads. And honestly, none of my current clients were concerned with the brand on my sign…they just wanted to make sure they got to continue working with me. New flag, new tools for me, business as usual for my clients.

Changing brokers prematurely when you have a history of job-hopping can stifle your forward progress and may have some root problems worthy of reflection. Remember, you take yourself with you, so the business issues you had with broker A can easily follow you to broker B. And if your I've-changed-brokers new elevator speech involves a little bashing of your former broker, let's just say there is little grace in that approach and grace goes a long way in this business.

Changing brokers multiple times, like having way too many employers on your resume, can handicap your business. Brokers will see your movement and want to know why. In most towns and cities, even in the large cities, the real estate community will feel smaller than you think. It is very easy for a broker to pick up the phone to get the scoop on you and your reputation. Are you leaving because of new business opportunity and vision, or because your broker is showing you the door? Each agent's reputation is an extension of the broker's reputation, and they will want to make sure you are a solid addition to their team. But bottom line, find your belonging place.

BROKERS AND CLIENT LEADS

It is pretty rare that your broker will simply hand you client leads like Halloween candy. Most agents with most firms will be in a position of building their own pipeline. This is the first reality of starting in the business, that your broker does not necessarily hand you clients; the most successful agents have little to no reliance on their broker for client leads. Take some time to understand what opportunities exist within the brokerage for lead generation and for leads to be distributed to agents, and if the commission split varies depending on the source of the lead or price point. A broker may have a split arrangement of 70/30 (you 70% of the commission, broker 30%) or 80/20 when it is your lead, or maybe higher once you are a superstar, but it's 50/50 if it is their lead. This has a big impact on your income projection and how many transactions you need to close in order to hit your target income for the year. Understanding how the brokerage handles these things makes sense at this stage of the game.

If there is a surplus of broker leads, new agents may get the bottom of the barrel...old leads, lease leads, lowest dollar leads, leads in a town an hour away. Brokers may spend a lot of money or have earned their reputation over many hard-worked years, so a lead that comes in will, in most cases, be assigned to an agent who has the highest likelihood of turning it into an actual client, and then converting that into an actual close and, thus, income for the brokerage. It's a business.

Broker leads can come from many sources. Yard sign call-ins, online clicks & registrations, walk-in traffic, phone duty, social media and e-mail campaigns, events, and other various marketing campaigns. These sources can be very helpful for new agents getting started, but keep this very important business principle in mind; the agents who consistently generate their own leads are almost always the highest earners versus those agents who rely on the broker. So do you want to be dependent on iffy leads from someone, or do you want to learn how to create your own leads so that you are in control of your business?

MORE THINGS TO CONSIDER

What is important to you with where you hang your license? It may be as simple as a holding place with low costs and no bells and whistles, or it may be the full monty foundation for your empire building. Let's take a closer look.

Reputation, It's Not What It Used To Be!

Broker reputation and training are no longer limited to a brick and mortar address. We live in a mobile world. A great many people conduct their digital lives on their phones now, not their computers, and certainly not by walking into an office on main street (except for maybe in a resort community, but those folks are online first). So find the company that will help YOU be the agent of choice. Ultimately, it's YOUR reputation, YOUR brand, YOUR following, YOUR ability to attract client opportunities!

Training: You Don't Know What You Don't Know

Your license classes helped you pass a test. But how will you learn the business? How will you become a contract expert? A market analysis pro? The ramp-up of your skills and knowledge base in your first few years is extensive. Truth, you are always learning in this business…is your brokerage set up to support that? Is your brokerage set up to train new agents? Perhaps more importantly, is your broker set up to train and develop talent? To help the new agent become the middle agent? To help the middle agent become the mega agent?

Training matters, and the reality is that most of it is online these days. YOU will learn without the limits of location (think CLOUD based). And take full advantage of classes offered by your local Board of Realtors, and your state organizations, and the plethora of what NAR has to offer online.

Culture Matters

What are the values of the brokerage? Is there a mission statement that resonates with you? Is it cut-throat, super competitive, expensive suits only, or is there an everyone-wins-when-each-of-us-succeeds environment? Is it low-pressure or high? Is it micro-manage or how-can-we-support you? Publicly owned, privately held, stock, profit share, revenue share, open books? Some of the best corporations out there attract and retain talent by culture first, service second, product third. Zappos, Apple, Southwest Airlines, REI, Whole Foods...these places feel good, the employees appear happy, the environment is up. Culture matters.

Space, Cloud, Conducting Business

Some brokerages are shifting to more of a virtual model. Virtual as in cloud-based, no office, work from home, figure out where to meet with your clients model. This keeps a brokerage's expenses low. Most agents do work from home, so this can make a lot of sense. If this is your model, you may be meeting a lot of clients at Starbucks or in their home, or maybe some shared workspace or at your lenders office or a title company conference room. This works for an increasing number of agents in our cloud-based world.

Or you may need a storefront. If you are in an area with a lot of walking traffic or where drop-in traffic makes sense, such as a beachside vacation destination, the visibility of a storefront on Main Street can be important.

Are there meeting rooms? Training rooms? Professional conference rooms? Copiers for agent use? Rentable office space for your team? In some cases, space matters. In many cases, it does not. For me, I work from home, I meet my sellers at their properties, and I meet buyers all over the place. I do most of my training online, but I do some in person, and I meet with colleagues in person once or twice a month to talk shop. Cloud works for me.

Marketing & Branding

Some brokerages will be very, very specific about your branding (it's their branding, not yours), and other firms will give you all sorts of leeway with how you market yourself, your signs, your outreach, and how you can or how the brokerage will regularly communicate with your database.

Let's talk about yard signs for a minute. You can gain more traction and opportunity from listings than you can from buyers. This is because listings usually include a yard sign and are the vehicle that puts your name all over the internet when that for-sale is syndicated, via your MLS or your broker, to hundreds of websites. So on the yard sign or the online listing, is it the broker's phone number or yours or both? Is your name on the sign? Is it more likely for a drive-by neighbor to call the broker's main office number or your cell phone directly? It is your listing in the neighborhood you grew up in, that you worked your tail off for a year following up and following up and following up and coaching your cousin or best friend or neighbor to get their home ready to go on the market and list with you, their trusted advisor. It's your listing. But in most states, it is technically the broker's listing. The broker owns the listing (and takes on liability for that contract).

The information on the sign and your ability to gain additional opportunity from that listing is huge for building your business and something to take into consideration when choosing a broker. There is an industry saying "list to last", meaning that the agents who have more sellers than they have buyers will have more pipeline-building opportunities, more staying power.

Let's talk about logos and branding for a minute. Can you have your own logo? Branding within the brand? I am The Nelson Project at eXp Realty. I am a brand within my brand with a dba filed with the county and with the Texas Real Estate Commission. My sign and marketing include both my personal logo and my brokerage logo, and has been approved by my broker. Not all brokers allow this...you use their sign and their logo, period. I figure I am building my business first and my broker's business second, so marketing flexibility is my preference.

Database Is Gold

I put this in here specifically right after marketing so that you can focus in on an important business detail. In real estate, you have two primary assets: your time and your database. Who you know, that relationship, and all their contact information, is the biggest asset in your business. Your ability to add to and communicate with your database will play a huge role in building your business and creating more and more opportunity, stability, and financial predictability.

So what is the broker's policy on your database? Do you own it or do they? If you leave the company (a pre-nuptial sort of mature question), do you get to take the database with you? Does the broker continue to market to those people? So if you left the firm, are all your friends, family, and former clients going to continue to receive regular emails from ABC Realty (without your name on it) when you now work for LMNOP Realty?

Technology, Tools & Resources

Speaking of database, does the broker have quality tools in place that allow either you or them to effectively e-mail blast the database with quality information or new listings or market updates? And is the brokerage providing that to you for free or a basic technology fee? There is usually a non-negotiable fee. Are they running online ads, do they have a social media presence, what tools do they provide? Is that important to you? You will have a ton of options with tools and software, some free, some with price tags. While some of these tools originate with your local board, agents tend to rely on their brokerage to lead the way in this arena.

Is your broker current? Are they using the same technology tools they were using fifteen years ago with a "seems to work for us" mentality, or are they evolving with the all-things-mobile business and consumer environment? Are you the techiest person in the firm and somewhat on your own, or does the broker lead the way? Again, what is important to YOU?

So what tools do YOU really need? Your needed-tools list will evolve, and the reality is that most brokerages or boards will pretty much provide some or most of the following:

- Customer Relationship Management (CRM) software
- Contract-writing software with electronic signature tools
- Some form of branded home-search website with your name on it
- A customizable listing presentation and other marketing material

Is it important to you that the broker provide these tools? As for me, I like a robust technology and marketing platform, and those tools could be expensive if I went out on my own to fill my basket. I like the power of leveraging the company to be successful. Make sure you can do that too. Most companies offer a technology platform (some more effectively than others). But make no mistake. They are just tools. YOU are the "product" that clients will be "buying".

Client Leads & Opportunities

Does the broker provide opportunity for you to gain client leads from within the brokerage or will you be solely responsible for all leads? Is that important to you? Broker opportunities may include phone duty opportunities, open house opportunities (holding other agents' listings open), and simply excess leads (someone clicking on the broker's website or calling on a sign around town). These "excess" leads may tend to be the lower end of opportunities as the broker, often his or her spouse, will take on the higher-priced leads. Is the broker a producing agent or a full-time CEO? Most brokers in the smaller and medium sized firms are also practicing (or many times their spouse handles all their clients) and will screen all leads that come into the brokerage...the broker gets the best, highest dollar leads, then will have some sort of process (is there a process or is it a bit arbitrary, possibly including favoritism?) to distribute the other leads to other agents. In most cases, the broker is going to distribute the lead to an agent with a proven record of converting leads into clients and clients into closed transactions. And you need to know what the broker split is on these broker-sourced leads. This broker split is often 50/50 on this type of lead, but I have seen it at zero.

Are They Hiring?

Not all firms take on brand new agents. Some firms only take on niche agents, such as luxury or someone fully networked in a certain part of town, or for smaller firms, someone they know. Most national franchises take on newly licensed agents and some of them specialize in that, with robust training and mentoring programs. If they take on brand new agents, do they have the training, support, and mentorship to back it up and what is the cost?

Cost Expectations

Besides licensing costs, which we covered earlier, here are some additional costs you may want to assess as you make a brokerage choice. Do you or does your broker provide and/or pay for:

- For-sale and open house signs
- Lockboxes
- Business cards
- E&O insurance
- Administrative support

HOW ARE BROKERAGES STRUCTURED?

Brokerages come in all shapes and sizes. Let's take a brief look.

The Mom and Pop

Mom and Pop real estate offices go way back in real estate history and there may be hundreds of them in your area. Some of these brokerages may have been in the same family for multiple generations, and some are very specialized. If it's your family, then it is most likely your landing place. Many of these are one to ten agent operations, some larger. Some of these have reputations for being way out of date, some are cutting edge.

The Boutique

This is a generalized term for, typically, small to medium-sized local market-specific brokerages. Some may have originated as a mom and pop. Many boutiques serve a specific neighborhood, sometimes a specific high price point, sometimes a niche market such as downtown condos. Maybe the boutique spreads their geographic wings to more than one office, often the boutique is one well-placed office.

The Local-only Firm

Realty Austin, Port Aransas Realty, these are very geographic name specific. They may have more than one location, but the geographic name may define them. They can be big players, especially in smaller towns.

The Big Brokerages

These are the big players, many of them franchised. Some are publically owned and traded, some privately held. You will find them coast to coast and, in some cases, internationally. From eXp Realty, to Keller Williams Realty, to RE/MAX, to Coldwell Banker, to Berkshire Hathaway (Warren Buffett, purchased Prudential), one or more of these may dominate in your market. The massive Realogy Holdings Corporation owns Better Homes and Gardens Real Estate, CENTURY 21, Coldwell Banker, ERA, and Sotheby's International Realty.

Franchise Big Office

There are franchise real estate offices that have over 500 agents. I was a member of one over 800. This rarely means that all those agents actually have a desk in that office; it means they hang their license there with that specific broker and address. This type of office can completely dominate a market by dominating listing inventory. But agent count does not equal agent productivity, which may be something for you to consider. These big shops tend to have big staffs and resources.

Franchise Not-so-big Office

Some franchise offices may have twenty or thirty agents. The models are different. Some franchises strive for a fifty-agent office; some franchises consider their break-even profitability line to be a minimum of 150 agents. Each of these offices will have their own personalities.

Publically Owned vs. Privately Owned

All businesses need to satisfy their owners with profitability. Sometimes the owners are the agents, sometimes the owners are the franchisees, sometimes the owners are the stockholders, sometimes it is a mix.

Cloud-based

This is a newer category and is a sign of the times. eXp Realty launched in 2008 and I think it deserves its own category. (Yes, I disclosed my bias earlier.) There may be other emerging players in this arena…I would expect that, as it is simply how we operate these days (hello Netflix, hello Uber). I will use eXp and me, personally, as an example. eXp has their headquarters in Washington state. My broker has a small office in Austin. I work online and from home and can meet my clients in their home (sellers), Regus office space, or at my favorite lender's office or Starbucks or pretty much anywhere or virtually. I have a network of fellow local eXp agents that I meet with in person, once or twice a month, to mastermind our businesses. I do all of my training and client process online and I access the headquarter services easily online (no commute). Cloud-based means that expenses are kept low (brick and mortar is very expensive for a brokerage office), so resources can be heavy loaded into services and technology.

Hybrids

Real estate is a big and evolving industry, and really big money (like really really big) is being pumped into development as I write this book. So if I were to outline today's hybrid brokerages, like a 100% brokerage or virtual reality brokerage or the latest discount brokerage option or what Zillow is up to today, that landscape would likely change by the time you are reading this a few years down the road. While hybrids have come and gone, especially over the last ten years, they can represent the cutting-edge and occasionally one stays.

If you lean geeky or dream about giant what-ifs for this industry, then sure, go to town on studying the latest industry trends and hybrid development in our great big world. But for the purposes of this book and your process of choosing a broker, in a relatively timely manner, understand your options in your city and get busy assessing which one is the best fit for you and your vision.

ACTION ITEM: ASSESS BROKER CHOICE

Pick which category you fit into, new agent or not new agent, and walk yourself through a somewhat methodical process of choosing the broker that works best for you.

Category 1: Broker Choice Assessment For New Agents

- Step 1. Write a list of what is most important to you in your first few years in the business. Assume massive success, identify what is most important to you in your brokerage choice.
- Step 2: Write a list of all the brokerages that interest you.
- Step 3: While you can certainly analyze every single brokerage, most of us do not have that sort of time. (Remember the over-analysis, getting-ready-to-get-ready discussions earlier in the book and how that can seriously slow you down?) Circle your top two or three brokerages from your list.
- Step 4: For your brokerage shortlist, gather information from numerous sources including directly from that brokerage (do they have a new agent page on their website? did a representative visit one of your classes in real estate school?).
- Step 5: Grade them on what is most important to you. Keep it simple. It may be yes, no, maybe, I-don't-know. Or plus or minus. Or A, B, C.

- Step 6: Talk with a few agents from each firm.
- Step 7: Set an appointment to visit with the brokerage manager or talk in-depth with the person you know at the brokerage. Ask questions, find the right fit, find your belonging place.
- Step 8: File an application.

Super Valuable Bonus Step In Your Brokerage Choice Process

Note: When I say "bonus" throughout the book, it is usually an indication that, when fully embodied and implemented, the bonus thing could actually result in generating business, building your pipeline, creating fans. Here is your bonus in the choose-your-broker process:

Stir the pot with your family, friends, and sphere and get ten of them on the phone or face-to-face and engage them on the broker choice or broker switch topic. Your conversation may go something like this:

> I want to run something really important by you, get your opinion. Do you have a few minutes to chat? (You can message them that to set up the call.) As you know (they should because you have been doing a good job of talking about what you are doing), I am very close to being fully licensed in real estate. I am beside myself excited about getting started! I have to decide on a broker and, before I do that, I wanted to run a few things by some of my most valued advisors, and you're on the short list. So I have a few questions for you…ready? (And then go through the conversational process of asking some or all of these questions.)

"When did you buy or sell your last property?"

"What was most important to you in that process?"

"Who did you work with at the time? What brokerage were they with?"

"Would you work with them again?"

"Have you worked with other Realtors?"

"How did you choose them?"

"Did you choose the agent or the brokerage or both?"

"If you were about to build a real estate business, what brokerage would you consider? Do you have any favorites around town?"

"Is there a broker you know and trust that I should consider?"

"Do you have any advice for someone starting a new business?"

"I have big goals for my business. When I get started, will you give me a shot?"

"I appreciate your support."

If you are an experienced agent considering changing brokers, do a similar version of this exercise with a few trusted friends. Tell them you respect them as level-headed business professionals and you would value their opinion on a business decision you are about to make.

Then send them a thank you note or a bouquet of flowers if they were amazing and generous and gracious in the conversation. You are pre-building your business...these conversations matter, and can often be the differentiating factor between the superstars, the rapid starters, the first-year success stories, and everyone else. Start heating up that pot before you have your license. Always be looking for opportunities to have quality conversations with your favorite people.

Category 2: Broker Assessment For Not New Agents

In my opinion, the broker assessment for a not-new agent is very different than it is for the brand new agent. For the currently licensed agent reassessing brokerage affiliation, we'll split this assessment into two important sub-categories, introspective and business. The grass may be greener, maybe not. You may simply be moving to another town and need to reassess, or you are just not happy and thriving where you are and need to fix that. Take your time, and work yourself through this process.

Introspection

Always start within. Take inventory and ownership of who you are being in your business. This is sort of the pointing-a-finger exercise. The finger you are pointing at your brokerage for something that is not a fit or not working—you know the exercise— there are four fingers pointing back at you and that is where we want to start. If you move to another brokerage, you will be taking yourself with you, so would you agree that it is possible, even highly likely, that your problems may follow you? Ask yourself these questions:

- Am I fully engaged in my business?
- How is my energy?
- Am I having fun?
- Have I fully engaged in what the brokerage has to offer?
- What do I like best about my brokerage, broker, office?
- Have my business needs changed?
- Has my brokerage or broker or office dynamic changed? And does it still fit?
- Did something specific happen or change, or has this been a gradual evolution of new or emerging needs and preferences?

- If I take my existing business habits and practices with me, is that okay, or do I need to step up?
- What is missing?
- What am I seeking?

Business

Positive pull or negative push? Are you considering changing brokerages or offices because a new opportunity is presenting itself? Or are you considering a change because something is not working in your current campsite? This is an important question. Rank your current needs regarding these business considerations:

- Leads & Sales Opportunities - The top line on an income statement is gross sales, income. Are there new or greater opportunities at the other brokerage and, if so, how will you qualify?
- Training - Are you getting what you need?
- Mentoring - Do you need more?
- Support - Are you getting the support that you need? And are you sure you will get it at place two?
- Tools - Are you missing some critical tools in your business and another brokerage can deliver?
- Environment and Culture - Ask most agents, and this is actually a biggie. In so many cases, your work environment and colleagues form a bit of a tribe, an extended family. Are you feeling the love? Is this your belonging place? Is there a values match? Are you feeling aligned with the overall message from the brokerage or is there a mismatch?
- Physical Location - Sometimes big-time important, sometimes not at all. What do you need?
- Specialties - Do you need a brokerage that supports a

specific specialty? Commercial, farm and ranch, leasing, new construction, waterfront?

- Costs - Yes, at the bottom of the list. Not every business decision is bottom line. If your sales increase significantly, do your cost concerns go away?

CHAPTER 17

WRAP IT UP WITH A BOW ON TOP!

Where does your money meet the meaningfulness of your life?
— Danielle LaPorte, *The Fire Starter Sessions*

SACRED PACT

I made a sacred pact with myself to make a difference.

The earliest version of this book was an ongoing newsletter. Then a series of blog articles, and then a self-published e-book that was more or less a brain dump of everything I had pieced together on the topic. If you have a book in you, start there.

I know from experience and from being a decent observer that success with a new endeavor, a new project, a new relationship, a new business, can simply change your life. And when you change your life, it inevitably changes someone else's life. It is a beautiful pattern of ascending meaning and value and trips to adventureland.

I have seen new parents succeed in real estate because it supported their vision of how they saw themselves parenting, how they envisioned their new family and their ability to be fully present and involved.

I have seen the newly divorced create financial independence and a new lease on life.

I have seen newish agents whose family history and personal experience was one of ongoing financial scarcity. Their upbringing, their family histories, their entire lives had an ongoing theme of financial instability. Their real estate success represented not only their personal financial freedom with savings, a decent credit score, and options, it represented a new vision for the siblings, the nieces and nephews, the next generation. Similar to the first child in the family with a college degree, this business success financial freedom thing would set a new standard, a new vision for the family.

Whose life and vision will your success impact? What difference will you make?

Even moderate success can change your life and change the world. Moderate success indicates that moderate plus is possible. And moderate plus indicates that massive success is possible. Success is incremental, it builds upon itself. Rarely linear, often a curvy path, sometimes success goes in reverse before it moves forward…remember the cha cha cha?

Here's the cool thing—you get to decide what moderate and plus and massive looks like for you. Success is personal; don't let someone else define it for you. You may define your success in financial terms, maybe in more personal lifestyle terms. Maybe you have something to prove. It's your goal and your life. My intention, my hope, my sacred mission, is that this book, this voice, and one small portion of the message is the catalyst, the nudge that may change your life.

INFLUENCERS

As I wrap up the writing of this book, I realize there are a number of books that provided grounding, guidance, direction, and enough success analogy material to fill a second edition. Each of these books alone can be transformational and I realize that I have been reading and rereading and referencing these gems for years. I would not be as confident or complete or balanced or clear or easy on myself today without them. Highlighted, dog-eared, post-it-noted, gifted to friends, these are working books. I have hard copies, Audible copies, notes, blog articles, and social media posts preaching their game-changer attributes. I have downloaded all of their free online material and resources. I subscribe to their mailing lists, I seek them out on YouTube, and have purchased some of their add-ons and upsells. For me, these are the game-changers, compass-setters, course-correctors, great equalizers that have influenced me, and I believe they can help you along your way.

Reading List

The Fire Starter Sessions: A Soulful + Practical Guide to Creating Success on Your Own Terms, Danielle LaPorte

The ONE Thing: The Surprisingly Simple Truth Behind Extraordinary Results, Gary Keller and Jay Papasan.

You: Staying Young: The Owner's Manual for Extending Your Warranty, Michael Roizen, M.D. and Mehmet Oz, M.D.

The Millionaire Real Estate Agent: It's not about the money, Gary Keller with Dave Jenks and Jay Papasan

First, *The Fire Starter Sessions: A Soulful + Practical Guide to Creating Success on Your Own Terms*. I want to be Danielle LaPorte when I grow up. At a time when I was questioning my path, evaluating my choices, scrambling for joy, and recalibrating my compass, LaPorte and her sassy savvy knocked me off my seat. Drop every self-help or career guidance book you've ever read, take them all to the used bookstore, and cozy your psyche right up to the gritty, kick-ass, stop-being-so-hard-on-yourself, embrace-what-you-love, career as passion-meets-ambition, church of Danielle

LaPorte. LaPorte is business meets soul.

The ONE Thing. If you have not yet read this, do yourself a favor and pick one up on the bestseller kiosk at the airport. The birth of the book started with this principle: "Whenever I had a victory or win, I realized I had narrowed my focus." And the foundational question in the book: "What is the ONE THING that I can do such that by doing it, everything else will be easier or unnecessary?"

Why is it that, given the same resources and the same amount of time in a day, some people achieve extraordinary results while others fall flat or give up? Keller and Papasan tell us that the principles outlined in *The ONE Thing* apply to almost everything, from how to get through college, to how to lose 20 pounds, to how to succeed in your chosen profession. This is one of those books you are going to want to highlight, watch videos, download material, take notes, gift to your friends.

You: Staying Young. I know, an unlikely finalist, but hear me out. I have been writing *Success Faster* over the span of a couple of years. If you have ever attempted to write something lengthy, you will relate to this concept. In the two-year span of writing and re-writing and developing this book, any other book or article I picked up had me thinking about writing style, anecdotes, and analogies for a healthy business. The *You: Staying Young* book by Roizen and Oz dumbs down, in a dummies-for-xyz sort of way, your health and your personal ecosystems. The book is a surplus store of analogies for a healthy business.

The Owner's Manual for Extending Your Warranty may as well be the owner's manual for having a decent chance of thriving or simply staying in this business called real estate. Our bodies and our businesses are great big simple and complex ecosystems, and stuff that happens in one department affects the results in another. Our bodies and our businesses are not just impacted by external things. More so, they are impacted by the choices we make on a daily basis, and who we are being in that body and in that business.

The Millionaire Real Estate Agent: It's not about the money, by Gary Keller with Dave Jenks and Jay Papasan, is pretty much a must-read for any Realtor. It is the business school model for building a successful real estate business. It is so widely used and referenced throughout the industry that it is often referred to as the MREA or "the red book."

I coached a new agent years ago who owned a few restaurants around Austin. He was in the process of selling two of them and assessing what to do with the third. He was obsessed with the MREA book. I remember him saying that if there had been the restaurant version of the MREA when he started in the services business, he would be a wealthy man today and would not be sitting in my office starting his next career. He was in his mid-thirties.

One more big influencer, perspective setter, and personal GPS is my personal collection of TED Talks. I am obsessed with TED Talks. My treadmill time typically involves a TED Talk, either on Apple TV or my podcast app on my phone. I listen and watch, and re-listen and re-watch. I watch TED Talks specifically related to this book, to business, mindset, achievement, happiness, a little science, music, design, and architecture. My treadmill time is often disjointed as I pause the treadmill and scribble a reference. Fast walk, pause, scribble, cardio, pause, Siri note, fast walk, pause, scribble. (I don't run.)

I watch these amazing inspired and inspiring Ted Talkers and hope that it eventually somehow even slightly may impact my habitual language, my mindset, my go-to statements of encouragement, and my grasp-this-for-business-development tips. At what point do these Ted Talk gems morph into my own language? I can only hope a few of them stick in the language center of my brain. I study my TED Talks notes like an athlete lifts weights; I'm on them all the time. I work on building my brilliance muscle, building my accessible Rolodex of encouragement and clarity. At the least, they feed my positivity; at best, I'm awesome at a cocktail party.

Honestly, it was not easy narrowing this list. Here are my TED Talks *Success Faster* influencer finalists:

Shawn Anchor, *The happy secret to better work*, May 2011 at TEDx

Isaac Lidsky, *What reality are you creating for yourself?* June 2016 at TED Summit

Brene Brown, *The power of vulnerability*, June 2010 at TEDx Houston

Meg Jay, *Why 30 is not the new 20*, February 2013 at TED2013

Elizabeth Gilbert, *Success, failure, and the drive to keep creating*, (also *Eat, Pray, Love*), March 2014 at TED2014

THE END.

Not really, you just started! Honestly, I don't think there is ever an end. And instead of perceiving that non-end concept as an endless loop or an exhaustion formula, I choose to think it may just be the secret of life and the secret to always moving forward and the secret to always creating something amazing in your life. There are cycles and rebirths and starts and restarts and launches and relaunches and it all adds up to this beautiful and sometimes gradual and sometimes not and sometimes small and sometimes massive but always inevitable evolution of you and your mission and your place on this great planet. When I have influenced you with just one small nudge in your evolution, then we are both in the right place at the right time.

Who else do you know who could use a little encouragement and a real estate roadmap? Pass it on.

I wish you joy and success in your journey.

Oh, one more thing. Earlier in the book, I said I would mention the chicken farm thing. My professional journey, of course, involves my personal journey. As I look back over the years and the various homes I have owned and the gardens I have developed (and honed and nurtured and sculpted and weeded), each address tells a story. With a dream, a decent track record of real estate investments (not all were perfect but some of them have been exceptional), a respectable track record of professional success, and a dual-income household, my spouse and I purchased three raw cedar-filled acres on the edge of Austin five years ago. (Side note: the property was not even on the market. We had been eyeing it, and our good friend lived next door, so we wrote a very personal letter to the 93-year-old owner and it all came together.) After a year of clearing and planning and building, we moved into our dream home, our modern farmhouse, with acreage to fill with gardens, dogs, and an amazing chicken coop full of hens. You may give wine and gift baskets to your clients, we give fresh eggs.

WHAT'S NEXT?

In the next series of pages, you will find the action item reference and an easy-to-access script reference. The action and script is where you do the heavy lifting of gaining clients faster.

And there's more. If you flip to the back of the book, you will see an online resources page with links where you can learn more and participate in conversations with other professionals who are on a similar journey. The main *Success Faster* landing page is www.career456.com, where you will find various resources, tools, articles, and links.

I am honored to deliver to this you…and then beyond blessed when something in these pages made a difference. Whether that difference-maker was big and life changing or simply a modest course-correction, either way, I have done my job.

ACTION ITEM REFERENCE (AND SOME SCRIPTS)

ACTION ITEM: Call Your Mother

Call your mother. Seriously, call your mother (or your sister or bff), and here's what you are going to say:

> *"Mom (sister, bff), I just started at [broker name] today! OMG, I am so excited! Wish I had done this earlier. I need your help. This is day one of the training program and the very first assignment they gave me was to call you! This business is seriously referral-based, and I have big goals. Will you help me? It's now my job to know the real estate needs of my friends and family and their friends and families, so there is a basic question, actually two questions, that I need to ask you. 1. Are you anticipating any real estate needs this year? 2. Is there anyone you know who may need my services this year? It's pretty much my job to ask this question, and who better to start with than you? I really super appreciate your support."*

ACTION ITEM: Identifying Your TOP 100

Get out your phone. Get your neighborhood list. Your church directory. Your Christmas card list. Your kids' school directory. Your former colleagues. Your golf league. Don't forget your family.

In town or out of town or out of state...all of them. Your college friends. I have brand-new agents who got their first or second client because they called their cousin or college friend halfway across the country. You know a LOT of people! Let's identify your top 100, because I promise you, there is business in there. Your immediate job is to cultivate and coax the leads out of that top 100 list.

ACTION ITEM: TOP 100, Calling

Call one to twenty of your TOP 100, and here's what to say:

> "Hey, Sam, it's [me]. Do you have a minute? I know you're at work, so I'll be fast. I wanted to let you know what I'm doing. I've thought about this for years, finally pulled the trigger, and I am now an associate with xyz Realty. Love it, wish I had done this sooner! So a couple of quick questions: 1. Do you have a go-to Realtor when you have a real estate question? [NO: Great, you do now! Or YES: Great, happy to be the second person on your list.] Second question: Are you anticipating any real estate needs this year or know anyone who may need my services? I appreciate you keeping me in mind. I'll send you an e-mail right away so you have my contact info. Everything good with you? Would love to do lunch or happy hour sometime, catch up. What's your schedule like the next couple of weeks?"

ACTION ITEM: Affordability Factor

You're talking to renters. Quickly, make a list of everyone you know who rents or probably has a lot of friends or colleagues who rent. If there is an employer in your town that hires a lot of millennials, figure out who you know who works there. I am in Austin, Texas, so this topic is a great tool for my 20-something and 30-something friends who work at tech start-ups downtown, or who work at Google, or Facebook, or Apple.

One way or another, figure out how to have this conversation with as many renters as possible:

"Oh, you're renting? Have you thought about buying? You know, interest rates are historically low. Like they'll never be lower. They will go up . . . not if, but when. Well, I thought of you this morning because I was thinking of this. Have you thought of buying? If you did buy, what neighborhood interests you?

"Your timing can be critical because when interest rates go up, let's say from 4% to 5%, that will impact how much home you could buy. If you qualified for that cute $250,000 home in Shady Grove today, you may only qualify for a $230,000 home next year. And prices are going up. I'd hate to see you miss the market, miss the opportunity to live in Shady Grove. Does this topic interest you? I thought so. Would you like to meet for coffee to talk about it more, or I can introduce you to a mortgage broker just to explore your options . . . which sounds better? Is there anyone else you know who is renting who should probably take a look at this?

"Hey, while we're on the topic, is there anyone you know who may need my services this year? We're already setting up appointments for this summer. Keep me in mind . . . I'd love the opportunity to help your friends and

colleagues. I'm going to shoot you an e-mail real quick so you have my info handy."

ACTION ITEM: Mondays!

Here's what to say to anyone with whom you've had a real estate conversation over the past few days or on the weekend:

"As I said I would, I just wanted to follow up on our real estate conversation from Saturday. Is this an OK time? Great. So tell me again what you're thinking, what your needs are. [Listen. Ask questions.]" Then set a timeframe for your next follow-up and e-mail something of value [maybe just a follow-up e-mail to recap the conversation, or possibly an article on the topic or a personal note]. Make a note in your calendar [or whatever system you're using, your CRM] for the follow-up.

Then ask this question (the POWER QUESTION which we will scuba dive into in the next chapter): *"Hey, real quick, while we're on the topic… Is there anyone else you know who may need my services this year? We're already setting up appointments for [summer] and I always want to make sure I am saving spots for my friends and their friends. Thank you for thinking about it. My business is primarily referral-based and I appreciate your support."*

Yes, tweak as necessary. Always tweak the scripts so it sounds and feels natural for you.

ACTION ITEM: CRM

Take 30 minutes and do a Google search for best Realtor CRMs. Read a couple reviews comparing them. Maybe ask your Realtor network what CRM they are using and what they like best about it. The other option is take 30 minutes and go over a couple tutorials or best-practices articles on the CRM you are already using, or is made available to you.

ACTION ITEM: Power Questions (PQs)

Read the PQs again and the how's-the-market responses out loud ten times fast. Another option is to pair up with another agent and plow through this exercise together. The goal of this quick exercise is simply speed and repetition. Speed and repetition. In fact, you may want to do this simple exercise every day this week and next week and the week after. Go over and over and over and over these questions. Speak them out loud, write them out on a notepad, type them out, record yourself on your phone, and listen to them in your car (hands-free, of course). Speed and repetition.

The call: Pick one of the PQs in this chapter and call someone, call five, call twenty...heck, walk your block and ask your neighbors. This is not an e-mail, it is not a post on Facebook. You must have conversations with people. Do not move on to the next chapter without this ACTION ITEM checked off.

ACTION ITEM: Your Calendar Is Money!

Five hours per week. Let's keep this really simple. Get out your calendar. Pencil in five hours per week of practice. Or more.

ACTION ITEM: CALL YOUR BIGGEST ADVOCATE, AGAIN

Sometimes our closest people can be our biggest advocates *and* our biggest critics. So the conversation may be as simple as giving that important person an update on how you're doing. It may look something like this:

> "Hi. It's me. I wanted to give you a little report of how things are going at work. I want you to see how serious I am and tell you a couple things I have going on. Got a minute?"

> "First, I really appreciate your support. So I [then go on to tell them about your open houses, the buyer you're working with, that as the national sales manager of your real estate business you basically go to the office in the morning and do not leave until you have talked with x number of people about real estate . . . or some pertinent fact about what you're doing]."

Then ask if you can practice a script or two with them over the phone.

> "So I spend about an hour a day just practicing what to say, my presentations, and studying the market. I realized I would like a little real feedback, trying to get this to sound natural. I want to run this by you, get your feedback."

Then practice with them. They may laugh a little; they usually offer a little advice like "be yourself," then half the time they'll mention someone who may have a real estate need.

You always want to end with a question, something like this:

"Is there anyone you have come across recently who mentioned real estate?"

And then you need to train them HOW to help you:

"When you do hear of someone, don't just give them my card. Instead, say this: "You know what? I really want to introduce you to/have you talk to my friend [your name]. She's the friend I mentioned who is a Realtor. What's your e-mail? I'm just going to send an e-mail that introduces the two of you. No pressure; she'll treat you like family and may be able to help you. At the very least, she'll be a good resource."

ACTION ITEM: Find Your Five People

Your top five people, get them on the phone. Here's what to say:

"I promised myself I would call you today. Do you have a second?

Option 1: *You know everyone. You probably know more people than anyone I know. That's why I'm calling. I have big goals for my business this year. Here's my quick and easy question: Who do you know that I should know?*

Option 2: *You love me, right? I need your help. I have big goals for my business this year. Here's my quick and easy question: Who do you know that I should know?*

Option 3: *You've started your own business/ you've accomplished some impressive things.*

That's why I'm calling. I have big goals for my business this year. Come have coffee with me. I want to ask you about your success, advice for starting something new. I figure I should listen to successful people and you're on my shortlist. What is your availability this week or next?"

Option 4: *How can I help you? You have always been very supportive of me and my business. How can I help you? How is your business? What are you working on? Is there anyone I know that you would like to meet? Let's have coffee and catch up.*

ACTION ITEM: Local Businesses

Pop in to ten local businesses and introduce yourself. This can be especially helpful when it is an area of town that you regularly visit or that you live in or near. Are you in a smaller town? Then stop by every single business. Focus on whatever it takes to get into conversations with people. And keep going back. Start building that recognition of you as Realtor, you as hard-working Realtor. Sometimes it is as simple as a "Hello, it's your favorite Realtor again!" What if you started meeting all your favorite people and connections in the same coffee shop all the time and you got to know the coffee shop owner and the staff?

Back to the pop-ins at the local businesses. Here's what to say:

"I live nearby, and I realized I did not know every small business in the neighborhood, so I thought I'd drop by and introduce myself. I am a Realtor who specializes in this area of town. Where do you live? Do you have a go-to Realtor? When you have a real estate question, who do you call? Do you have any

real estate needs this year or know someone who could use my services? Here's my card in case you hear of someone. Do you have a card? I appreciate your time. I'll stop by again. I like this place. What's the one thing I should know about your business? [listen] Great. I am going to send some business your way. Have a great day."

And note, you may want to buy something while you're there, if appropriate. That may work best for the coffee shop or gift store or auto parts store, not so much for the car dealership. But speaking of car dealerships, when I bought my Mini Cooper in 2010, my sales guy, Charlie, turned into a client.

And then go back and go back and go back. And send a friend or two or three in there and make sure they mention you with some form of, "My good friend Susan the Realtor sent me."

ACTION ITEM: Start Your Bio Document

ACTION ITEM: Your Fav

Find your Favorite

Review all the ACTION ITEMS in each chapter (and there is an ACTION ITEM reference section near the end of the book). What did you like? Identify one ACTION ITEM that you really enjoyed. And then double down on this. Whatever you enjoyed the most will most likely produce the most opportunity. If all of your leads are coming from friends, then call friends today with this:

"Hey, it's [me]. Got a minute? I realized all my business so far has come from friends or their friends. It's the thing I like most about the business. In order to hit my goals this month, I need two appointments every week. Who do you know I should talk to?"

If you have had FSBO luck so far or you just like talking to for-sale-by-owners, try this:

> *"Hey, Mr. FSBO. It's John with ABC Realty. I specialize in helping FSBOs get their homes sold, so I wanted to check in and see how it's going, see if you have any questions. Can you tell me a bit about the home? Are you familiar with the two required disclosures for sellers? At what point do you think you'll consider hiring a Realtor for the job of selling your home? (I have a sign in my car right now. We could have the home on the market in no time.)*

ACTION ITEM: Identify Your Procrastination

What did you miss? Identify one ACTION ITEM from the book that you either did not do (for whatever reason) or fell short on. Is there something you have said you would do, but it remains untouched? Sometimes it is just a matter of building more skill in that particular area and then results start to show up. Run with one of the items you have been avoiding and get more conversations under your belt.

ACTION ITEM: Your Calendar And My True Story

- Block one hour every day Monday through Friday and call it "practice."
- Set a recurring appointment with at least two of these daily practice appointments where you are practicing with another agent.
- Tell someone about this plan, this task, this goal. Someone in your household works nicely or a good friend or family member or your broker. Tell them that you are telling them so that they'll help you stay accountable.

- Print out a two-month calendar and post it on the wall somewhere. For every day that you hit your appointment, highlight the day.

ACTION ITEM: Write It Down

If you have not yet done so, put some words down in your journal addressing the following:

- What success looks like to me:
- What success will do for me and my family:
- My financial goals are:
- My personal goals are:
- My five-year vacation plan is:
- Here's how I will change the world:
- My sacred mission is:

ACTION ITEM: Assess Broker Choice

Pick which category you fit into, new agent or not-new agent, and walk yourself through a somewhat methodical process of choosing the broker that works best for you. Refer back to the chapter for the specific outline.

SCRIPT REFERENCE

Script Disclosure

The origin of most of these scripts is unknown. A few of them are my originals, or modifications of scripts I have adopted and trained on over the years from many classes, many sources, many hours spent on YouTube and various online Realtor forums. I paid very close attention to NOT copy and paste from any copyrighted material. Ever. Understanding the origin of the majority of real estate scripts is like wondering about the origin of your favorite chocolate chip cookie recipe...they have been around for a very long time and have become our language. You should modify them to best fit your needs and authentic style.

COMMON OBJECTIONS

What is your response to these basics?

- Why should I hire you?
- I think we'll wait.
- Will you lower your commission?
- We're talking to two other Realtors.
- I have a friend who is a Realtor.
- We want to price it at $325k (when it's worth $290k).
- We want to offer $30k below the list price (when it's the coolest home and the market and homes are selling for full price in three days).
- We're just looking.
- We're going to try to sell it by ourselves first.
- We're not ready to talk to a lender.

Why-should-I-hire-you?

My favorite response:

> "Maybe you should, maybe you shouldn't. I need to know more specifically what your needs are to make sure I am the right person and can deliver. You're interviewing me and I'm interviewing you; it needs to be the right match. What is your situation?"

BASICS

The Basic Lead Gen Script

> Version 1: "Let me ask you a business question real quick … are you guys anticipating any real estate needs this coming year? We are already setting appointments for first quarter and want to make sure we have you on our radar. I wouldn't be doing my job if I did not ask you this question every now and then."

> Version 2: "I know you know a number of Realtors. I just want you to know that it is my goal to earn your referrals. Just planting the seed. So what's the most important thing that you value in a Realtor? While we're on the topic, are you guys anticipating any real estate needs this year?"

LISTINGS

Listings, stick to your program:

"Mr. & Mrs. Seller, the more we stick to our program, the more I can predict and control the outcome. Any deviation from this plan simply moves us from the A+ plan toward the B plan; I can give you the best results with the A+ plan."

Listing questions to ask (having an online questionnaire will save you a lot of time, then at the listing appointment you are simply verifying the information):

- *What is most important to you in this process?*
- *What is the best feature of your home?*
- *What is the best feature of the neighborhood/location?*
- *What upgrades or improvements have you made?*
- *Is there anything positive or negative about your house or neighborhood that could affect the price?*
- *Do you have any deferred maintenance?*
- *What is your budget to get the house market ready?*
- *Pricing / financial:*
    - *What do you think the value of your house was at the peak of the market?*
    - *What do you think the value is today?*
    - *What is the price you will not go below?*
    - *Do you have a mortgage balance on the home?*
    - *Is there a second mortgage or are there any liens on the property that will need to be paid upon sale of the property?*
    - *Do you need the proceeds from this home for the purchase of your next home?*
- *Are you familiar with how buyers determine value in this area? Let's take a close look at that.*

POWER QUESTIONS

- *Is this the only home you have to sell or are there others?*

- *Is there anyone else you know who may need our services?*

- *What else do you need to see from us that can help you move forward with your plans?*

ONLINE RESOURCES

SUCCESS FASTER ONLINE

Find resources, material, and downloads here:
www.successfasterbookclub.com

456 COACHING CLUB FACEBOOK GROUP

www.facebook.com/groups/456club

JULIE'S AUSTIN, TEXAS REAL ESTATE BUSINESS

www.thenelsonproject.com

JULIE'S COACHING AND TRAINING BLOG

www.thenelsonproject.org

FOLLOW

Follow Julie Nelson and The Nelson Project and the 456 Coaching Club for future updates to this guide as well as best practices for new and emerging REALTORS®. If it is social and media, chances are you'll find me by searching *The Nelson Project* or thenelsonproject; in the case of Twitter, follow *@julienelsonATX*.

OBLIGATORY STUFF

ABOUT THE AUTHOR

Julie Nelson and The Nelson Project Inc. created this guide to help REALTORS® and other entrepreneurs succeed. Julie Nelson is a nearly twenty-year veteran of the real estate industry, including a five-year assignment running one of the largest new agent broker training programs in the country.

Julie is an active Realtor with eXp Realty in Austin, Texas. Thenelsonproject.com is Julie's real estate business, thenelsonproject.org is Julie's training and entrepreneurial blog. Julie lives on her somewhat urban farm in Austin, Texas with spouse, Kay, three old dogs, one cat, two miniature donkeys, and fourteen or so chickens. When not doing real estate stuff, you will find Julie in her gardens or on her bike.

This publication, *Success Faster: Quickly Launch or Relaunch Your Real Estate Career*, and subsequent publications or products distributed or sold are in no way affiliated with any particular real estate broker, brokerage, or franchise. All information within these pages is the creation of Julie Nelson and The Nelson Project Inc. Copyright © 2017.

DISCLAIMERS AND DISCLOSURE

This book is not intended as financial, legal, or broker advice. Regulations, standards, license requirements, and license ethics may vary in your area, region, state, or brokerage. Licensed REALTORS® must consult their broker for legal, client and contract advice. Unlicensed (pre-license) folks cannot give the impression that they may be licensed and, thus, cannot take the majority of actions outlined in this book. Acting like a licensed real estate agent when you are not licensed is illegal. Know the rules in your state, learn the nuances in your area. The author does not take any responsibility for the results of your actions as prescribed in this book.

The author is legally and ethically bound by the standards and ethics of the NATIONAL ASSOCIATION OF REALTORS® and the Texas Real Estate Commission, and personally bound by the golden rule. The author, Julie Nelson, is a licensed REALTOR® in the State of Texas.

USE OF REALTOR®

A note on the National Association of Realtors® (NAR) trademark, the ®: For readability purposes, I include the REALTOR® in the first reference in each chapter and omit it in the rest of the document. NAR says we can do this. REALTOR® is a federally registered collective membership mark which identifies a real estate professional who is a member of the NATIONAL ASSOCIATION OF REALTORS® and subscribes to its strict Code of Ethics. This book is intended for REALTORS® and those considering real estate as a career.

REALTOR® CODE OF ETHICS

The NATIONAL ASSOCIATION OF REALTORS® Code of Ethics has been in place since 1913. A lot has changed since then. The code changes with time and is updated annually. You can read the NATIONAL ASSOCIATION OF REALTORS® Code of Ethics in its entirety at www.nar.realtor/code-of-ethics.

NOTE PAGES FOR YOU!

NOTE PAGES FOR YOU!

NOTE PAGES FOR YOU!

NOTE PAGES FOR YOU!

NOTE PAGES FOR YOU!

Made in the USA
Coppell, TX
27 February 2020